IMAGES
of America

HOWARD COUNTY LAW ENFORCEMENT

On the Cover: The gangster era of the Depression paved the way for innovation in the Kokomo Metropolitan Police Department. The second car from the left in this photograph, taken on the north side of Kokomo City Hall in 1932, is fully armored with heavy plating, bulletproof glass, and a gun port in the passenger side of the windshield. (Courtesy of Jon Zeck.)

IMAGES
of America

Howard County Law Enforcement

Tom Kelley

ARCADIA
PUBLISHING

ISBN 978-1-4671-1265-9

Published by Arcadia Publishing
Charleston, South Carolina

Printed in the United States of America

Library of Congress Control Number: 2014951970

For all general information, please contact Arcadia Publishing:
Telephone 843-853-2070
Fax 843-853-0044
E-mail sales@arcadiapublishing.com
For customer service and orders:
Toll-Free 1-888-313-2665

Visit us on the Internet at www.arcadiapublishing.com

This book is dedicated to the memory of Indiana State Police first sergeant and Miami County sheriff John A. Rusie (pictured), who showed me everything I needed to know about being a good policeman. (Courtesy of Maj. Matt Bilkey, Indiana State Police.)

Contents

Acknowledgments

Some 30 years ago, Howard County sheriff's deputy Jon Zeck became interested in the story behind his local public safety agencies. This snapshot of policing in Howard County, Indiana, was his idea. It never could have happened without him.

Then Craig Trott, another retired deputy, came along with an immense collection of crime scene and accident photographs, which he had taken throughout his long career, and other vintage photographs depicting the sometimes funny, sometimes tragic working world of Howard County police. Unless otherwise credited, all of the photographs in this book were provided by Craig, to the exacting standards of our acquisitions editor, Jesse Darland.

Throughout my research for this book, a great many other people have been helpful. Around kitchen tables and often with a good Irish whiskey within reach, they shared their scrapbooks, stories, and perspectives. Their professional experiences represent the very foundations upon which the Kokomo Police Department, Howard County Sheriff's Department, and Indiana State Police function and breathe life into some of these images. Thank you, Matt Bilkey, Butch Braden, Andy Castner, Don Cloum, Steve Daily, Larry Darlin, Dick Ferguson, Marty Getz, Jim Goerges, Gary Guest, Charlie Hackett, Jerry Harrison, Janice Hart, Don Howard, Larry Ives, Norris Jones, Jeff Kirk, Dave Kellar, Henry Melton, Tom Melton, Susan McKinney, James Moffitt, Flo Pogue, Steve Rogers, Lynn Rudolph, Bob Sargent, Jill Scott, Jim Stitt, Cliff Stover, Marty Talbert, Phil Templin, and Jay Weir. I hope that I have done justice to your contributions.

While this project enjoyed the full support and cooperation of the Kokomo Police Department and Chief Robert A. Baker as well as the Howard County Sheriff's Department and Sheriff Steve Rogers, any opinions expressed are my own and are generally unpopular with others.

Special appreciation goes to former and current *Kokomo Tribune* photographers Brian Reynolds and Tim Bath and the late Glen Banner, along with managing editor Jeff Kovaleski, for opening up their archives for this project.

This history of Howard County law enforcement was made possible by the men and women who created it.

The Law Along the Wildcat

The need has always existed, even in the most peaceful of societies, for men and women of good character, unflinching courage, tremendous emotional strength and patience, and compassion to step forward and do the unpleasant work that nobody else can or is willing to do. Whether an officer is known today as a deputy, a cop, five-0, a police officer, a pig, a trooper, heat, or a smokey, for the law enforcement agents in Howard County, the lineage predates the founding of both the city of Kokomo and Howard County.

The 500 or so people who originated the region now known as Howard County seemed indifferent toward the idea of political structure. Most everybody lived in settlements along Wildcat Creek or one of its tributaries, and white settlers barely outnumbered the Miami Indians in the area. But seeing a need for law and order, the governor appointed Jesse Barnett in 1837 as Richardville's first sheriff. One of the last counties in Indiana to be recognized, Richardville County was authorized by the Indiana General Assembly in 1844 and elected John Harrison its sheriff. But the Miami Indians had their own government, their own rules, and pretty much took care of their own problems.

Peter Cornstalk was one of about 200 Miami Indians who inhabited Howard County, mostly clustered around Wildcat Creek in the late 1830s. According to Owen Freeland's *History of Ervin Township*, he was known as an "honest Indian," meaning that he did not steal, partake of hard liquor, or get mixed up in any brawls. With his wife, he made his home in Ervin Township. He was walking home one night when he became ill and was later discovered dead on the trail. His friends, according to Miami custom, buried him with his gun, a tomahawk, some silver, and beads northwest of where County Road 1150 West now intersects with State Road 22 and where a stream, Pete's Run—named in his honor—runs into a fork.

The next evening, Sam Loon and another man arrived to rob the gravesite, but they were interrupted by Pete Jr. Loon was killed on the spot, and Pete Jr. tracked the second man for two years before shooting him near Joshua Barnett's Mill, which was located near 600 West and Old Sycamore Road. Freeland notes, "People questioned the law for not interfering," but they were told that Indian justice had prevailed.

In 1937, local historian Ed M. Souder wrote of those days:

> While Kokomo was in the formative period it was its misfortune to possess a considerable number of citizens of turbulent tendencies. These, in the main, were the backwash from the surrounding settlements. They saw to it that something exciting went on every day—at least every night. Everybody was on the lookout for something larky all the time. Assignations, hanging-bees, barn burnings, tar and feather parties and similar diversions came along with amazing regularity. Occasionally, just by way of variety, there was a little counterfeiting. Now and then public property would be destroyed. Once a brief period of comparative calm was broken by the barbequing of the County Jail. At a later period part of the equipment of the courthouse was purloined, carted away and deposited in a local stone quarry.
>
> Such was Kokomo in the good old days of town pumps, toll gates and Tom and Jerry tubs. Whiskey was plentiful and roughhouse abundant. The town did things with thoroughness even that early. Whenever it staged a riot, it did the thing up with all the embroidery that becomes such enterprises. It always invited the coroner to hang around in the background. Nothing was more certain than that there would be need for his services.

The first railroad came to Howard County in 1853, and the community's future as a commercial center was assured. However, 11 years passed before Kokomo became a real town with a real mayor and a real marshal. In the years following the Civil War, Kokomo's only depot stood at the junction of the Lake Erie & Western and the Panhandle Railroads, west of Main Street and south of North Street. "The Junction," as the neighborhood came to be called, was home to many of the town's brothels and taverns and was host to a level of rowdiness that exceeded the standards of the rest of the unruly community. One of the Main Street taverns was owned by Mart Mollihan, a Kokomo native and war veteran who had served with a US Army doctor named Henry Cole. The two remained friends after the war, and Mollihan persuaded Dr. Cole to open a practice in Kokomo.

The March 31, 1876, the *Kokomo Saturday Tribune* reports that Jesse Kelly, "who acts as night police," was stabbed in Mollihan's saloon during a fight with Charles Hawkins. A son of city marshal Joseph Kelly, Jesse died of his wounds the following July and, tragically, became the first Howard County law enforcement officer to lose his life in the line of duty. Kelly is buried in Pete's Run Cemetery, located on 125 North Road, east of 1250 West in Ervin Township. The next day, two Kokomo policemen rode the train to Nevada in Tipton County and arrested Hawkins at his father's house. A mob surrounded the officers while they waited with their prisoner for another train to take them back to Kokomo. Any attempt to free Hawkins were discouraged by the armed officers.

Thomas W. Lannon was hanging around the depot and talking with friends on a warm August evening the following year when Michael Gillooley snuck up behind him and fired a bullet through his head and another into his back. According to *Kokomo Tribune* articles that reported the shooting, Gillooley killed Lannon in revenge for interrupting his visit to a local brothel and placing him under arrest. A series of articles in the *Kokomo Tribune* the following September and October identified Lannon, 28, an Irish Catholic and member of Father Mathew's Total Abstinence Society, as having been "put on the police force" the previous May and "served efficiently and honorably."

With such an environment of lawlessness, it is not surprising that, in 1880, the good citizens of Kokomo elected an accused murderer as their mayor. Dr. Henry Cole had gained a wide reputation as a surgeon of rare ability in the Union army. A tall and exceedingly handsome man with tiny hands, Dr. Cole dressed impeccably and wore a magnificent beard. He was, Kokomo historian Fred Odiet has written, "a fascination among women."

Nellie Cole was the doctor's first wife, and, when she began secretly courting Chambers Allen, the doctor threatened Allen's life. In October 1866, Dr. Cole shot and killed Allen in front of the post office on Buckeye Street near Walnut Street. Cole was arrested for his crime and later tried in Tipton County following a venue change. The good doctor was back in Kokomo two months later, having been acquitted after a plea of emotional insanity.

Entering public life did nothing to change the physician's practice of burglary, intimidation, and arson. In September 1881, Sheriff James DeHaven learned of a plot to rob and burn the Spring Mill, which was on Jefferson Street near Indiana Avenue. As a result, two constables were deputized to assist Deputy Sheriff J.W. Learner in a stakeout of the mill. The officers surrounded the place as best they could at about 9:00 p.m. An hour and a half later, two men climbed into the mill through a window and began handing sacks of flour to a third man outside. The deputies closed in, and, when one of the men fled, they dropped him with a hail of buckshot. Moving in closer to see who they had shot, they found Mayor Cole, lying on his back with a revolver in each hand.

Of course, that was not the end of it. After the shooting, Mayor Cole's supporters claimed that Sheriff DeHaven and his deputies had entered into a conspiracy to assassinate the mayor. The most popular theory in this conspiracy was that the mayor had been lured into the country, was murdered, and that his body was delivered to the mill, where the burglary scenario was played out. No evidence, however, was every produced to support this theory.

The following year, Richard Long was arrested for assaulting a child. While he was being held for trial in the jail at the southwest corner of what are now Washington and Superior Streets, a gang of masked vigilantes broke him out and carried him to the Main Street Bridge spanning Wildcat Creek. As a makeshift gallows was being arranged around a girder in the bridge, Long denied his guilt. As a last request, he asked to be able to sing a tune. Not being in any particular hurry, the hanging party granted his request and then listened to a folk song of the era, "See that My Grave Is Kept Green." As the last notes faded into the night, somebody pushed him off the bridge.

Just a year after that event, two men rode into town and tried to sell their horses to Nelson Cooper, who owned a local livery stable. A deputy sheriff had seen the men and became suspicious when they tried to sell their mounts. As they were being questioned, one of the horse thieves drew a revolver and shot Cooper dead before turning the revolver on the deputy and firing a wild shot. His bullet missed the deputy but struck John Lowe, who died an hour later. The two horse thieves turned their horses to flee, and the shooter was thrown from his saddle and then shot by a well-intended citizen, at which point the murderer surrendered. His accomplice got away. Identifying himself only as Jones, the 26-year-old man was held in the jail until the night of June 3, 1863, when a mob used a battering ram to get him out. Taken to a crude scaffold, Jones blamed his actions on alcohol and then was quoted in the *Kokomo Tribune* as saying, "I pray that God may not attribute murder to those about to execute me without form of law." Then some boxes were kicked out from under his legs.

While the City of Kokomo had appointed a marshal since its inception in 1865, the Kokomo Metropolitan Police Department was not chartered by the state legislature until March 1901. Chief Ross Taylor commanded a police department of six men who were further governed by three appointed police commissioners until 1951, when they were replaced by the Board of Works and Safety. Police headquarters was located in the City Building at Walnut and Washington Streets until 1983. A uniform and badge, sidearm, and a sturdy pair of shoes were all the equipment these early officers needed to fulfill their responsibilities. Within 20 years, the police department would acquire a motorcycle and touring car, and manpower was quadrupled.

By the 1930s, two passenger railroads served Kokomo, so coming and going was made pretty easy. Whether it was the ease of travel, Kokomo's lovely women, or just the idea that Kokomo was out of the way, something appealed to Harry Pierpont in 1925. Pierpont had lived in Indianapolis, Fort Wayne, and Toledo, but he often stayed in a boardinghouse at the corner of Madison and Washington Streets with Madge Keller, who owned the place and lived on the premises. Ordinarily quiet and soft spoken, Pierpont, along with Thaddeus Skeer and Roscoe Hayes, terrorized three employees of the South Kokomo Bank on the northeast corner of Markland and Market Streets. According to the March 27, 1925, *Kokomo Tribune*, the trio relieved the bank of $4,828 in cash and another $6,300 worth of bonds and securities. They were arrested in Detroit after Fort Wayne police received a tip about Skeer's girlfriend. She was watched as she boarded a Detroit-bound train. Her description was sent to the Detroit police, who were able to follow her from the depot to the robber's hideout, where all three men were arrested and extradited back to Kokomo.

While awaiting trial, Skeer married his girlfriend in the front room of the courthouse and was then handed a 10-to-21-year sentence. Pierpont drew the same sentence, and the charges against Hayes were dismissed. Pierpont and two other men escaped from the Indiana State Prison eight years later. While in the prison, they had met John Dillinger, and on October 12, 1933, they freed Dillinger from a Lima, Ohio, jail after killing the sheriff in his office. Later the same month, they robbed the police stations in Auburn and Peru of weapons, ammunition, and bulletproof vests. The Dillinger Gang was back in business. Former Kokomo policeman and sheriff Bob Sargent believes that Dillinger was hiding out in Nellie McCormick's boardinghouse in the 800 block of North Main Street while he planned the police station robberies. All four men were arrested in Tucson a few months later. Dillinger, of course, escaped from the jail in Crown Point, Indiana, and was later killed by the FBI in Chicago. Harry Pierpont tried to escape from the Ohio State Penitentiary, where he was awaiting execution for the murder of the sheriff. He was wounded in the attempt but survived the shooting and was subsequently and successfully executed by the State of Ohio in 1934.

The United States entered World War II on December 7, 1941, and its young men went off to fight the fascists in Europe and the Pacific. A relative calm fell over Howard County while the Depression eased and war rationing took over. Residents spent their days supporting the war effort and tending victory gardens, while their evenings were spent around the radio, listening to world events. By 1942, the size of the Kokomo Metropolitan Police Department had again doubled, to more than 40 men. In 1945, the Kokomo police hired 11 veterans. These men created a legacy of leadership and service that exists in Howard County law enforcement to this day.

This little book is a tribute to all the men and women of the Kokomo Police Department, Howard County Sheriff's Department, and Indiana State Police who have placed the safety of Howard County residents above their own fortunes, comfort, and well-being. These officers, deputies, and troopers have, for more than 100 years, been there for people on the worse days of their lives, when no one else would come and when no one else could help. Let none of us forget what they have done.

—Jon D. Zeck
Howard County deputy sheriff, retired

One

The Story You Are About to See Is True

The Early Years

People sleep peacefully in their beds at night only because rough men stand ready to do violence on their behalf.

—George Orwell (attributed)

Just about the time Kokomo's natural gas boom flickered out, the city decided that it needed a police department. In 1901, the governor of Indiana appointed three local men to serve on a board of police commissioners and to assist Mayor Macy Brouse in the formation of a new and, hopefully, improved Kokomo Metropolitan Police Department. As a result, four men were hired as patrolmen, another as captain, and Ross Taylor was appointed superintendent. The city marshals and their small band of hand-picked officers had struggled against counterfeiters, procurers, swindlers, and drifters to keep order in the rowdy community since 1865, with mostly unsatisfactory results. Much was expected of the new policemen.

The police commissioners understood Kokomo's troubles and what had to be done to fix them. The men they hired for the new police department had to be unfailingly honest, come with a good reputation, and, most importantly, be able to whip anybody who challenged them on their beat. Reputations were made early in those days, just as they are today, and a cowardly policeman, or a brave one who could not handle himself, did not last long. These men were up to the task. The violence in the Junction neighborhood was quieted in a few months, a number of grifters were run out of town, and several whorehouses were raided and closed.

A scandal broke out 10 years later, when Supt. George Windoffer accused one of his officers of insubordination and tried to have him fired. Nobody was going down without a fight, and the officer countered that his chief was providing protection for a hotel that was illegally serving liquor and prostitutes, not particularly in that order. When the evidence was finally aired publicly, everybody seemed pretty disappointed. The police commissioners suspended both officers and replaced Windoffer with Chief Melvin Gross.

Kokomo mayor Henry Cole was shot and killed by sheriff's deputies in 1881 while burglarizing the Spring Mill. Cole's supporters accused Howard County sheriff James DeHaven, who was nowhere near the mill at the time of the incident, of having the mayor assassinated. No evidence was ever produced to support the claims. The mill stood near the intersection of Indiana Avenue and Jefferson Street. (Courtesy of Elizabeth Kelley Cierzniak.)

Howard County's third jail (pictured) was constructed at Main and Superior Streets in 1893–1894 for the whopping sum of $34,000. The first jail had been built along Wildcat Creek on the grounds of what is now Foster Park. It was burned to the ground by gin-fueled hooligans just for the entertainment. The second jail had been on the southwest corner of Washington and High (now Superior) Streets. (Courtesy of Jon Zeck.)

Howard County built its first courthouse, a 24-foot-by-24-foot log-hewn structure, in the south half of what is now Courthouse Square in 1845. It was contracted for the sum of $28, but $2 were deducted from the fee for poor workmanship. Shown here is the fourth courthouse, erected on the same site in 1870 at a cost of $97,584.40. This building was considered more in keeping with the county's wealth and standing. (Courtesy of Elizabeth Kelley Cierzniak.)

The Kokomo Metropolitan Police Department acquired its first motorized vehicle in 1916. The paddy wagon is a Haynes Light Six Sedan that was modified in the Haynes plant on Lindsey Street to include the box bed. The term *paddy wagon* is a derogatory reference to the Irishmen who made up a large percentage of American police departments in those days. Chief Barney Kelly (far left) and Matron Mable Conkle are pictured here. (Courtesy of Jon Zeck.)

The 1916 Kokomo police motor fleet included a 1915 Harley-Davidson. Seated in this photograph are Sgts. John McNutt (far right) and Ira Lane. Capt. Omer Main (third from right) and superintendent of police Chester Miller are standing in uniform next to the paddy wagon, which was called Black Maria. (Courtesy of Jon Zeck.)

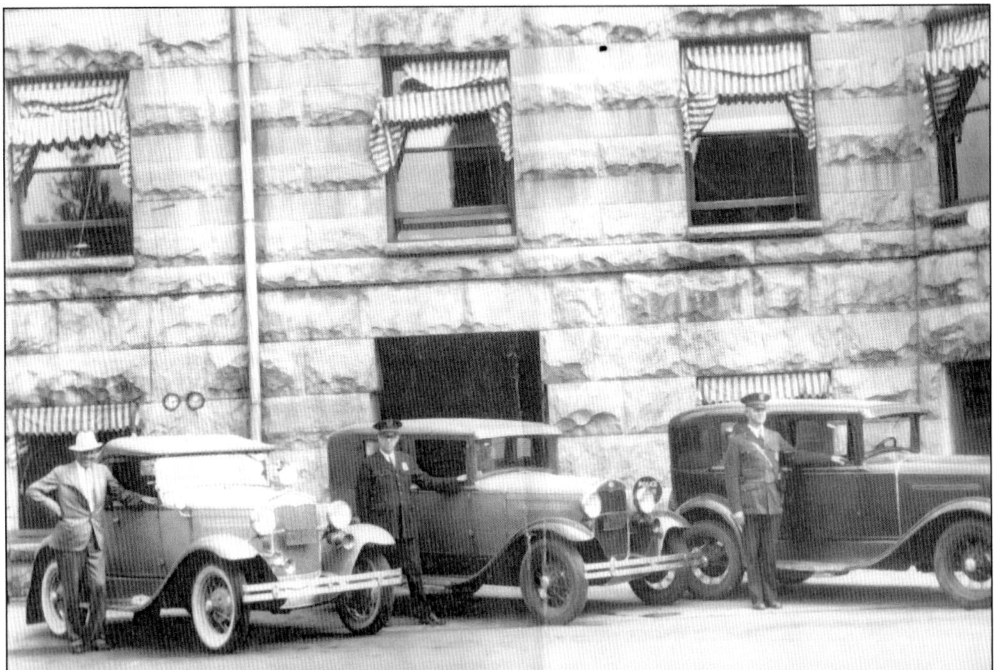

Chief Rollie Benson (center) was appointed in 1928. A devout Lutheran, Benson tried to build cohesion in the ranks by ordering his officers to shake hands at roll call. The tradition remains today and symbolizes the commitment Howard County officers have toward each other. Mayor Henry Quigley is on the far left in this photograph, taken in front of police headquarters. The man at right is unidentified. (Courtesy of Jon Zeck.)

Kokomo policemen march toward Markland Avenue on Union Street in 1925. Before the Police and Fire Pension Act of 1925, policemen competed with each other politically as well as competently to keep their jobs. Officers submitted their letters of resignation at the end of each administration, and it was up to the new superintendent or the mayor to determine whether they remained policemen. (Courtesy of Jon Zeck.)

The present courthouse, built on the site of the first one, was dedicated in October 1937. In a souvenir book printed for the occasion, Ed Souder proposes "that this goodly new home of public administration shall never be permitted to become the abode of either the corrupt or the incompetent and that it shall be entrusted in no part to any except the upright and efficient." (Courtesy of Elizabeth Kelley Cierzniak.)

One night, two men came into the police station. When the desk sergeant noticed that the younger man was bleeding, he asked what had happened. "Mr. Henry shot my son and told me to bring him down here, he's under arrest for something." Officer Henry Wagoner policed the "Negro" community from 1936 until 1958. His 1988 funeral in Three Rivers, Michigan, was attended by the entire local police department. (Courtesy of Jon Zeck.)

Sgt. Don Hale presents the national colors during opening ceremonies at the 1947 Policeman's Ball. The annual fundraising dance was held in various venues around Kokomo over the years, including the American Legion Hall at Taylor and Kennedy Streets (renamed Apperson Way in 1955). Officer Louie Love is marching behind Sergeant Hale. (Courtesy of Jon Zeck.)

Answering the need for something more efficient than separate, small, and untrained police departments, the legislature, in 1935, changed the Indiana State Highway Patrol into a state police force with general criminal jurisdiction and a fleet of modern, radio-equipped patrol cars. (Courtesy of Indiana State Police.)

"Ya gotta love cops," SSgt Floyd Talbert (actor Matthew Leitch) observes in the HBO miniseries *Band of Brothers* when, on the eve of D-day in June 1944, he receives a Colt .357 magnum revolver as a gift from the Kokomo police chief. While the incident is not included in Stephen Ambrose's historical account of the 506th Parachute Regiment, researchers for the miniseries learned from living Band members that Talbert said the handgun he carried throughout the war had been given to him by the Kokomo police chief. At the request of HBO, then inspector Dave Kellar learned that Chief Clinton Jackson was rumored to have given the handgun to Greentown native Talbert—but Jackson was police chief from 1940–1943. Floyd's brother Bob Talbert told historian Craig Trott that he and John L. Harper bought the handgun and shipped it to Europe. Harper would later become the Greentown marshal and serve until 1978. Floyd Talbert died in California in 1982. (Courtesy of Jon Zeck.)

In this 1947 photograph of the Kokomo Police Department, patrolman George "Al" Berryman (12th from left) and patrolman Henry Waggoner (13th from left) are standing in the first row. Both of these officers would go on to make local police history. (Courtesy of Jon Zeck.)

Kokomo policemen joined members of the fire department to host the first benefit ball in 1935. Policemen had organized the David Foster Lodge of the Fraternal Order of Police (FOP) by the end of the decade and hosted the popular event annually until 1983. (Courtesy of Henry Melton.)

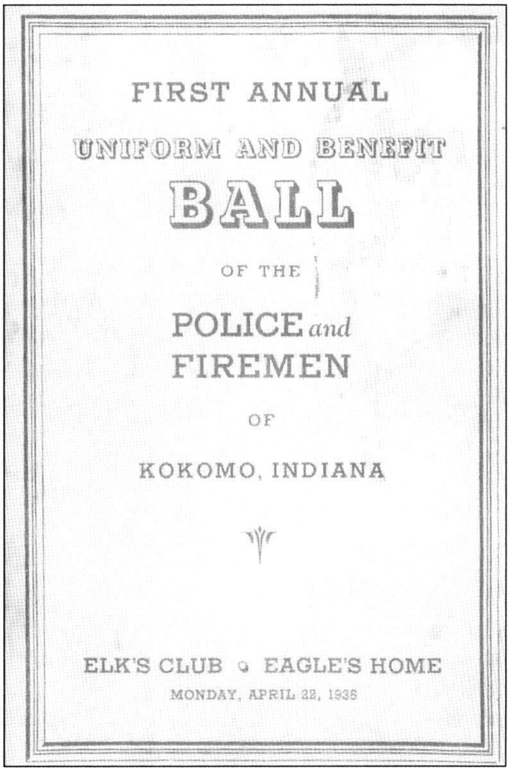

The Annual Policemen's Benefit Ball was held in the Kokomo National Guard Armory in 1948. This building on North Washington Street often served as a community center. It was vacated when the Guard moved to larger quarters at Markland and Home Avenues. (Courtesy of Henry Melton.)

After World War II, 16 veterans joined the Kokomo Metropolitan Police Department. Disciplined and motivated to continue moving their country and their community forward, these veterans established a legacy of leadership that lasted throughout the century. Here, the veterans, perhaps in police uniform for the first time, lead a parade on West Walnut Street. (Courtesy of Jon Zeck.)

Officer Obie Spencer was embarrassed to realize that he did not know how to correctly spell Deffenbaugh Street for his accident report. So, he dragged the dead horse over to Main Street. Spencer is seen here, the big guy second from left, in the squad room at police headquarters. On the far left is officer Wes Newton, whose family founded and still owns Kokomo Glass. (Courtesy of Jon Zeck.)

Two

A New Generation of Leadership

The 1950s

In this job you don't want to owe anybody anything. Next time pay for your own coffee.

—Patrolman George "Al" Berryman

When World War II was over, the Kokomo Metropolitan Police Department replaced nearly the entire staff with returning veterans. Between 1945 and 1948, thirty-eight new officers were hired. These men had tasted leadership or at least knew what to expect from an effective leader. They were disciplined, mostly ambitious, and many of them had experienced combat. When these men shed one uniform for another, they brought these qualities to the police department. George Berryman was one of them.

Bob Sargent was a fresh recruit in 1951 when he was paired with a more senior officer on the midnight shift. While patrolling on one very early morning, they found a door open at a Superior Street car dealership. After a careful search, they determined that an employee must have not properly locked up. The senior officer ordered Sargent back to the car. A few minutes later, the officer came out of the building, his arms loaded with car accessories. He dumped them into the backseat of the police car and disappeared again inside the building.

About that time, Berryman walked up and asked Sargent what was going on. The rookie officer, anxious to be accepted into the brotherhood but sickened by what he had witnessed, was evasive and nervous in his response. He no longer knew who he could trust; maybe the whole outfit was a bunch of crooks. Berryman walked around the patrol car and looked in the backseat. Then he, too, disappeared inside the building. When he emerged a few minutes later, the training officer gathered the stolen parts from the patrol car and took them back inside the building. He and Sargent rode the remainder of the night in silence.

The following night, Sargent reported for roll call and found his training officer absent. "He doesn't work here anymore," the shift sergeant said when Sargent asked. The rookie was then assigned to somebody else.

Patrolmen George "Al" Berryman and Harold Braden responded to a family fight call at 1201 West Mulberry Street on November 26, 1953. Vetha Spears had called the police from a neighbor's house and said that her husband, Archie, had tried to choke her after coming home drunk. Berryman is third from the right in the third row of this 1947 Kokomo Police Department composite photograph. (Courtesy of Jon Zeck.)

As the two officers approached the house, Archie Spears fired a shotgun blast at them through the screen door, killing Berryman instantly. Spears was killed seconds later by Braden's return fire. Both officers were posthumously awarded the Kokomo Police Medal of Valor in 2005. Lt. Harold W. Braden retired from the Kokomo police in 1969 and died on 3 October 2001 at age 73. (Courtesy of the Braden family.)

A Kokomo policeman prepares to lead a procession of antique cars along the new US 31 bypass in 1950. Designed as a limited-access highway, the bypass would become cluttered with shopping malls, restaurants, and side streets over the next 40 years, giving rise to Kokomo's moniker as "Stoplight City." This photograph was taken south of Boulevard. (Courtesy of Jon Zeck.)

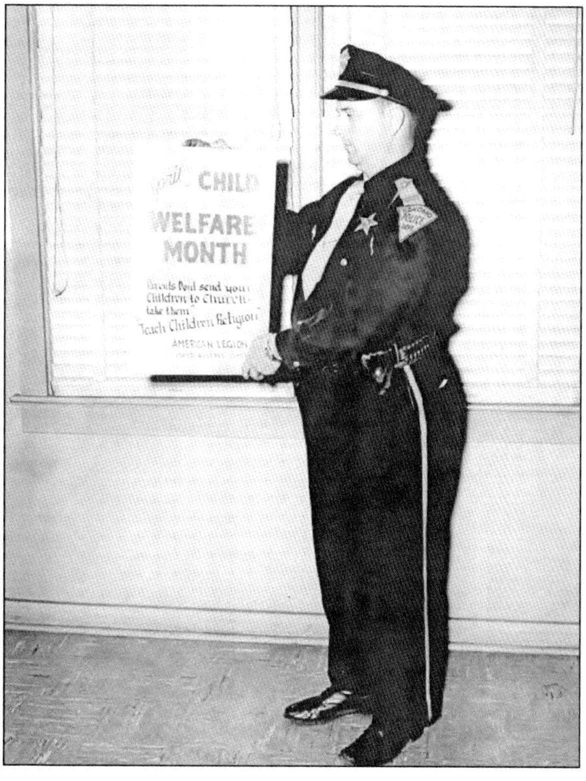

Officer Spence Huffman promotes Child Welfare Month in the early 1950s. Police chief Don Scott changed the uniform badge from a shield to a five-pointed star in 1952. He also permitted his officers to wear light blue uniform shirts in the interest of comfort during summer months. (Courtesy of Jon Zeck.)

Officer Charles Conwell and Sgt. Les Sosbe are prepared for midnight shift duty in 1953. The revolving emergency roof-lights were innovative at the time and replaced a static red light and siren combination. The mechanical, rotary sirens drew so many amps from the car's six-volt system that the headlights would dim during emergency runs. Ralph Pitzer's Shell station near Washington and Sycamore Streets is in the background. (Courtesy of Jon Zeck.)

Kokomo policeman Les Sosbe stops traffic for a funeral procession outside Memorial Park Cemetery on a cold afternoon in 1954. Businesses that routinely relied on police services, like funeral homes, law offices, and wrecker services, sent gifts to officers at Christmas. The practice was discontinued in 1980, when Chief Rodger Fain issued a policy forbidding officers from accepting gratuities. (Courtesy of Jon Zeck.)

Trooper Darrel Needler is on the scene in Alto after a driver lost control of a car and ran into the side of Luther Haynes's Citgo service station. In the 1950s, the Howard County sheriff employed only a few deputies, who were mostly responsible for running the jail and executing the business of the courts. Consequently, the rural areas of Howard County received police services from Indiana state troopers.

The notion that young drivers could be shocked, sickened, and terrified into adopting safe driving practices was reflected in training films like *The Last Date*, *Signal 30*, and *Anatomy of an Accident*. In 1958, local police contributed with a twisted display on Main Street across from the courthouse. Deputies Phil Plumber (left) and Pete Dieterly (right) are pictured with officer Everett Hurley (center). (Courtesy of Jon Zeck.)

The world-famous Budweiser Clydesdales are escorted along Buckeye Street near Jefferson Street by officers Les Sosbe and Don Petit in 1956. The usual Dalmatian seems to have been temporarily replaced by a chimpanzee, riding on the beer wagon with the driver. (Courtesy of Jon Zeck.)

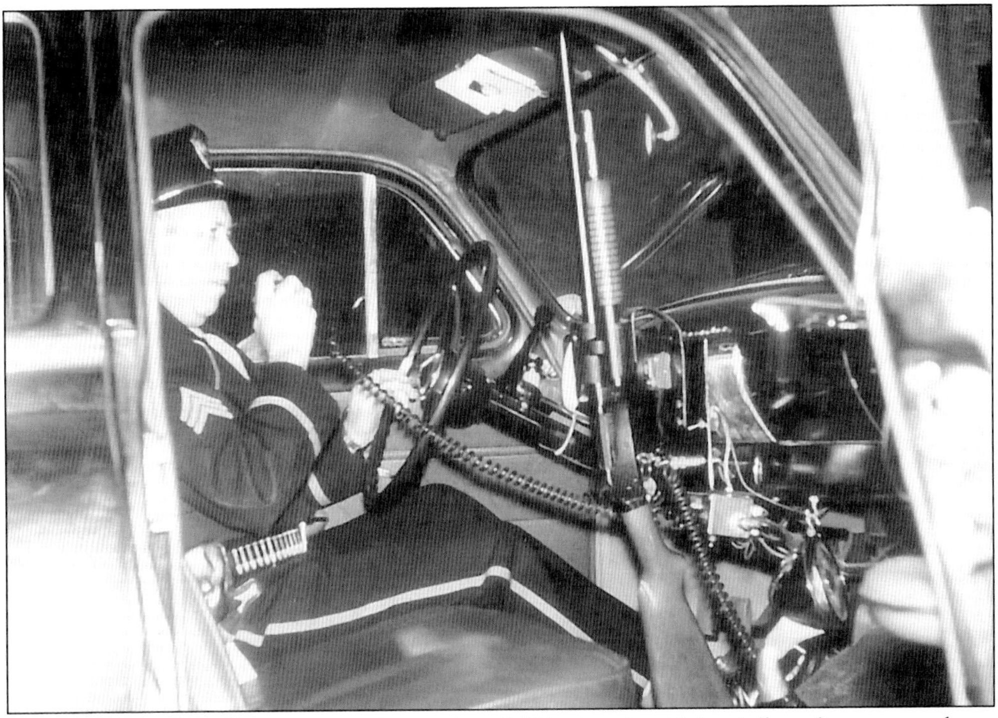

Former Los Angeles policeman turned writer Joseph Wambaugh said that "all a policeman needs are common sense, compassion and a sense of humor." But Les Sosbe seems to appreciate the high-tech tools that are afforded to him in a modern Kokomo police patrol car. Police cars today are so filled with computers, weapons, and cameras that there is barely room for a front-seat passenger.

An Indiana state trooper wearing jodhpur trousers of the era assists a deputy sheriff at an accident scene on US 31. The view in this photograph faces south between Center Road and State Road 26. Kokomo Harley-Davidson now stands in place of Rudy's Motel (far right).

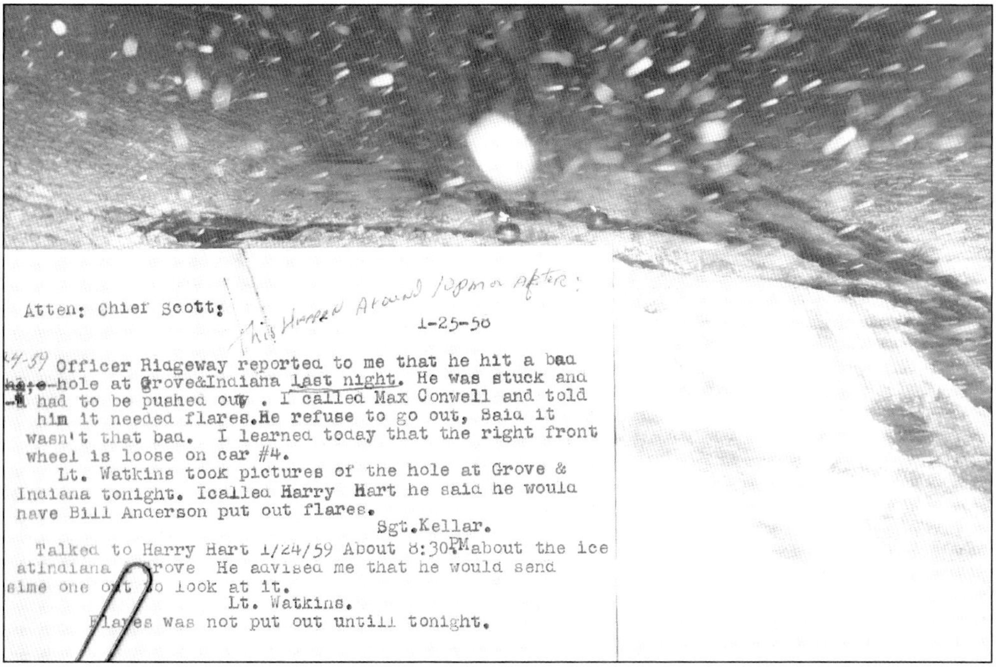

Midnight-shift sergeant Ray Kellar has explained in a note to Chief of Police Don Scott that officer Bob Ridgeway drove his patrol car into a huge pothole at Grove and Indiana Streets. This unfortunate incident occurred around 10:00 p.m. on January 25, 1958, and it was made worse when the street department refused to set out burning kerosene-filled pots, used to warn motorists of road hazards. (Courtesy of Henry Melton.)

US 31 had just been upgraded to a four-lane divided highway when this serious accident occurred adjacent to the Indian Heights subdivision. Indian Heights was developed to answer the need for family housing of airmen arriving at the new Bunker Hill Air Force Base.

An Indiana state trooper and a Howard County sheriff's deputy work together to investigate a vehicle rollover accident at County Road 600 East and 50 North.

A lone Indiana state trooper, in summer uniform, investigates an accident at County Road 300 East and State Road 22.

Kokomo police officer Les Sosbe is blocking traffic for a parade at Superior Street and Apperson Way. (Courtesy of Jon Zeck.)

Sears manager R.J. Lembke (left), Kokomo High School principal O. Farmer (center), and Howard County Civil Defense director Dayton Fortner test a Geiger counter during the Cold War. Howard County Civil Defense placed these instruments at designated fallout shelters throughout Kokomo to monitor radioactive fallout in the event of a nuclear attack. (Courtesy of Janice Hart.)

Howard County deputies Tom Leap (left) and Phil Plumber (right) walk a pair of prisoners into the courthouse. Deputies have transported inmates from the jail and deposited them on the west side of the courthouse since 1937. The Lincoln Finance building on the left of the alley across the street served as offices for the Kokomo Police Department Criminal Investigation Division from the 1970s until the police department moved into its current home at Sycamore and Union Streets in 1983. (Courtesy of Jon Zeck.)

Three

HOPE AND RAGE
THE 1960S

We don't know, but we can tell you one thing. If anything starts, it will be the cops who start it. Something has got to be done about that white man's army.

—Anonymous man at Monroe Street and Apperson Way

On a warm, Palm Sunday afternoon in 1965, a horrific tornado cut a wide swath of devastation from Russiaville, through the southern part of Kokomo, and then on to Greentown. The storms claimed the lives of 13 Howard County residents. As a result, the Town of Russiaville appointed its first marshal. Another seven residents died in a horrific and unrelated explosion at Stellite.

Sheriff Elwood Luellen worked closely with Indiana legislators in 1969 to establish a merit system for sheriff's deputies. The law protected deputies from arbitrary firing with each new administration and opened the door for a more professional, career-service deputy.

The 1960s, especially the late 1960s, were a period of turmoil in America. Young people, it seemed, were mad about the war in Vietnam, the military draft, civil rights, women's rights, Indian rights, pollution, unemployment, the arms race, haircuts, poverty, and every other sin committed against the freeman by anybody over 30. When people in the racially segregated Watts neighborhood of Los Angeles heard about a white California highway patrolman roughing up a black kid, they burned their own neighborhood to the ground. In the ensuing turmoil, 34 people were murdered and over 1,000 were seriously injured. A subsequent study "identified the root causes of the riots to be high unemployment, poor schools, and other inferior living conditions for African Americans in Watts."

Across the country, law enforcement had little patience with hippies, who responded by dropping out of society, and with the more radical and violent factions who were determined to change the American system of government by whatever means necessary. Events escalated during the 1968 Democratic National Convention in Chicago, pitting protestors against Chicago police in what looked on network television to be a massive incidence of police brutality. People were sickened and demanded police reform.

The enormity of these events rippled into Howard County and Kokomo on a hot night in June 1969, when a cross-burning touched off a violent race riot that left 14 Kokomo policemen and a state trooper wounded by gunfire.

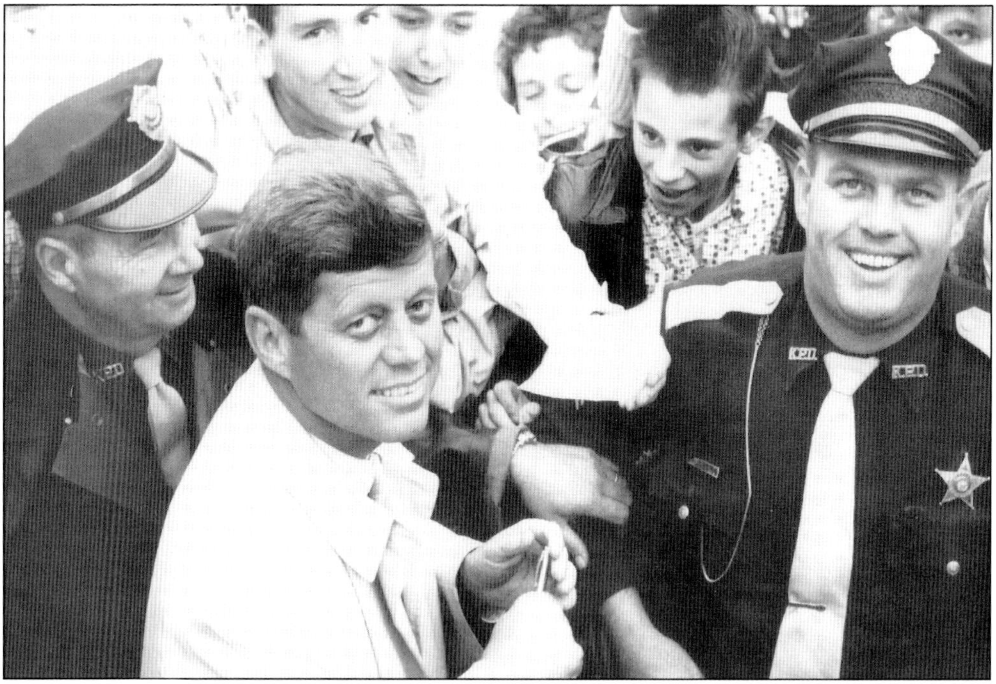

Officers Hale Watkins (left) and Chuck Sosbe (right) hold back an exuberant crowd while Sosbe and Massachusetts senator John F. Kennedy moon for the camera. The presidential hopeful received a warm Kokomo welcome on a cold April day in 1960. Sosbe would serve as police chief in 1971, and Kennedy was, of course, elected president of the United States. (Courtesy of Debbie Pearcy.)

The threat of nuclear war terrified everybody. The sheer power of nuclear weapons and the increasing likelihood of such an attack on the United States changed forever the role of civil defense. Something previously considered an important and commonsense asset, civil defense also became divisive and controversial in the charged atmosphere of the Cold War. (Courtesy of Janice Hart.)

Despite a general agreement on the importance of civil defense, Congress never came close to meeting the budget requests of federal civil defense agencies. Howard County Civil Defense volunteers made do with military-surplus vehicles and equipment. Here, volunteers pose with their impressive fleet of repainted Army trucks, cars, and motorcycles during a fair at the Kokomo Speedway. (Courtesy of Janice Hart.)

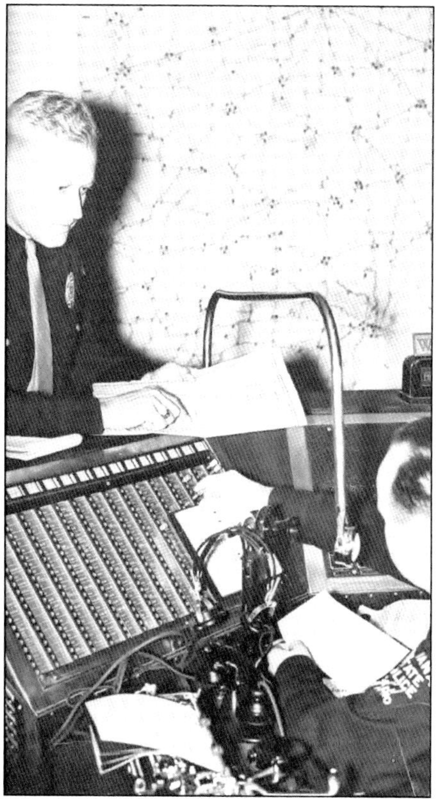

A state police radio monitor was installed at the Kokomo police radio tower because Peru Post went off the air at midnight, leaving Howard County troopers with nobody to talk to. Troopers would often call out in the blind, requesting a wrecker or ambulance and not knowing whether or not the Kokomo police dispatcher had heard them until somebody showed up. This hit-and-miss system worked remarkably well. (Courtesy of Indiana State Police.)

Deputy Sheriff Pete Dieterly (second from left) had already started investigating this traffic accident at Sycamore Street and US 31 in 1963 when trooper Jim Goerges arrived on the scene.

Sheriff's Deputy Pete Dieterly (in road) and Indiana state trooper Ed Hudson (in hat, behind car) investigate a rural accident involving a Chevrolet Corvair in 1963. Published in 1965, Ralph Nader's *Unsafe at Any Speed: The Designed-In Dangers of the American Automobile* dedicates an entire chapter to the Corvair and accuses car manufacturers of ignoring safety features like seat belts.

Deputy Phil Plumber directs traffic around an accident on State Road 26 at County Road 350 East. A trooper, whose patrol car is visible at left, is talking to somebody in the front seat. The white Chevy on the right is a sheriff's car driven to the scene by Pete Dieterly, chief deputy for circuit court.

Many of the accident photographs collected for this book, such as this one showing a scene at US 31 and Markland Avenue, were taken by Deputy Pete Dieterly.

Troopers investigate a 1964 crash on West Sycamore Street. This stretch of State Road 22 near Fire Station No. 5 was annexed into the city in 2007.

In his 1965 appraisal of public safely standards, *Unsafe at Any Speed*, consumer advocate Ralph Nader writes: "For over half a century the automobile has brought death, injury, and the most inestimable sorrow and deprivation to millions of people. With Medea-like intensity, this mass trauma began rising sharply four years ago, reflecting new and unexpected ravages by the motor vehicle."

The 1965 Palm Sunday tornado outbreak is reported to have been the deadliest storm in Indiana history, spawning 47 tornadoes and claiming the lives of 137 Hoosiers. One tornado struck Russiaville at 7:30 p.m. and completely devastated the community. The tornado remained on the ground and leveled structures across south Kokomo and then in Greentown. Here, a Honey Creek Township fire truck from Russiaville has been damaged. (Courtesy of Marty Talbert.)

Concerns about looting triggered the mobilization of Indiana's Army National Guard by Gov. Roger Branigin. In this photograph, the Greentown American Legion Post opened its doors as a shelter for survivors and a command post for troopers and Guardsmen. Incidents of looting were rare in the wake of the terrible storm.

Emergency services from the surrounding communities poured into Greentown, Kokomo, and Russiaville. Here, a field kitchen is set up along the sidewalk at Main and Meridian Streets in Greentown by the Indiana National Guard. Volunteer firefighters from the Cass County community of Galveston take a break from rescue efforts for a quick meal.

Luther Haynes ran flashing red lights on top of the wrecker he used from his Citgo service station. He figured that, as a legally sanctioned special deputy sheriff of Howard County and a self-appointed town marshal of Alto, he was entitled to an emergency vehicle. Marshal Hayes was the only law enforcement officer with a "shoot on sight" looting-prevention mandate after the tornado. (Courtesy of Elizabeth Kelley Cierzniak.)

The deadly Palm Sunday tornado inspired Greentown to purchase and build a community-wide storm warning system. Here, town marshal John Harper (right) and Greentown minuteman Don Flook examine concrete bases that have been poured for the mortar tube that was designed to fire a huge bottle rocket. The concept was that in the event of severe weather the marshal would run around town, presumably in a thunderstorm, and try to light off fireworks that would theoretically warn the townspeople. If the marshal could get the wet fuse lit, nobody could tell the difference between the explosions and the thunderclaps; still, the system was not abandoned until 1978. The Greentown Minutemen, forerunner of the Greentown Special Police, consisted of local volunteers who augmented the marshal's office during emergencies.

Northbound traffic had stopped for a Nickel Plate Road freight train on US 31 south of Lincoln Road when this Mercury station wagon slammed into the back of a waiting car in 1966.

Officer Dave Andrews (left of center) interviews a witness to a traffic accident at Home Avenue and Hoffer Street while rescuers help firemen load a victim for transport to the hospital. Capt. Larry Grecu is standing behind the ambulance on the right of this photograph.

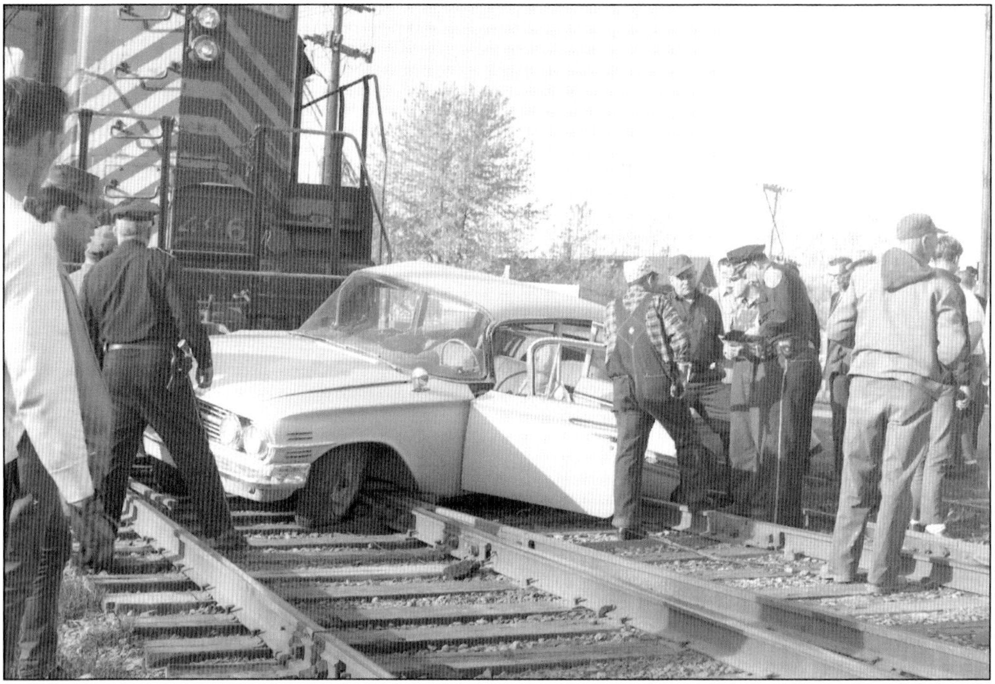

Kokomo police patrolman Dick East collects information at the scene of an accident involving a Nickel Plate Road locomotive. The car was struck at Havens Street but was shoved almost to Madison Street before the train could be brought to a stop. Police Chief Ray Kellar is also at the scene.

An Indiana state trooper investigates a vehicle accident at Alto Road and US 31. T-Way Plaza was on the northeast corner of the intersection, and the Hi Mark Restaurant was across the road. Other than the South Drive-In west of this intersection, there was little else to separate town from country. The Kokomo Gas and Fuel tower is visible in the background, more than a mile away.

Kokomo police captain Andy Castner (far left) confers with Indiana state trooper Ed Hudson during the investigation of a traffic accident at Sycamore Street and US 31. Hudson left the state police in the early 1970s and joined the Kokomo police. His son Tom Hudson also served with the Kokomo police before joining the ATF as an agent.

A late-night crash brought at least six law enforcement officers to US 31 and Center Road. Recognized in this photograph are, from left to right, trooper Darrel Needler and deputies Bob Biddle, Pete Dieterly, and Bill Emry.

Little thought must have been given to traffic congestion on West Markland Avenue when Continental Steel filled both sides of the street. A combination of heavy thoroughfare traffic, pedestrians, a truck terminal accessible only by backing in from the street, and no less than five busy rail crossings contributed to almost daily mishaps around the hardworking factory. Here, patrolman Ron Beaver investigates a crash at Markland Avenue and Lindsay Street. (Courtesy of Craig Trott.)

The Hi Mark Restaurant, seen in the background of this photograph taken at Alto Road and US 31, was a popular dinner spot for policemen because owner Mark McQueary never closed—well, almost never. When McQueary shut the doors for Thanksgiving and Christmas in the early 1960s, he arranged for police cars to be parked next to the building so the doors, which did not have locks, could not be opened.

Kokomo police officers direct traffic around a 1963 accident at Markland Avenue and US 31. Trooper Jim Goerges had only been out of recruit school a month when he was called upon to investigate this crash. He remained in Howard County until being promoted to a command position at the Peru District.

Officer Walt Baldwin investigates a traffic accident involving a motorcycle at Southway Boulevard and Lafountain Street in 1963. Sergeant Baldwin succumbed to that most deadly of police diseases 10 years later.

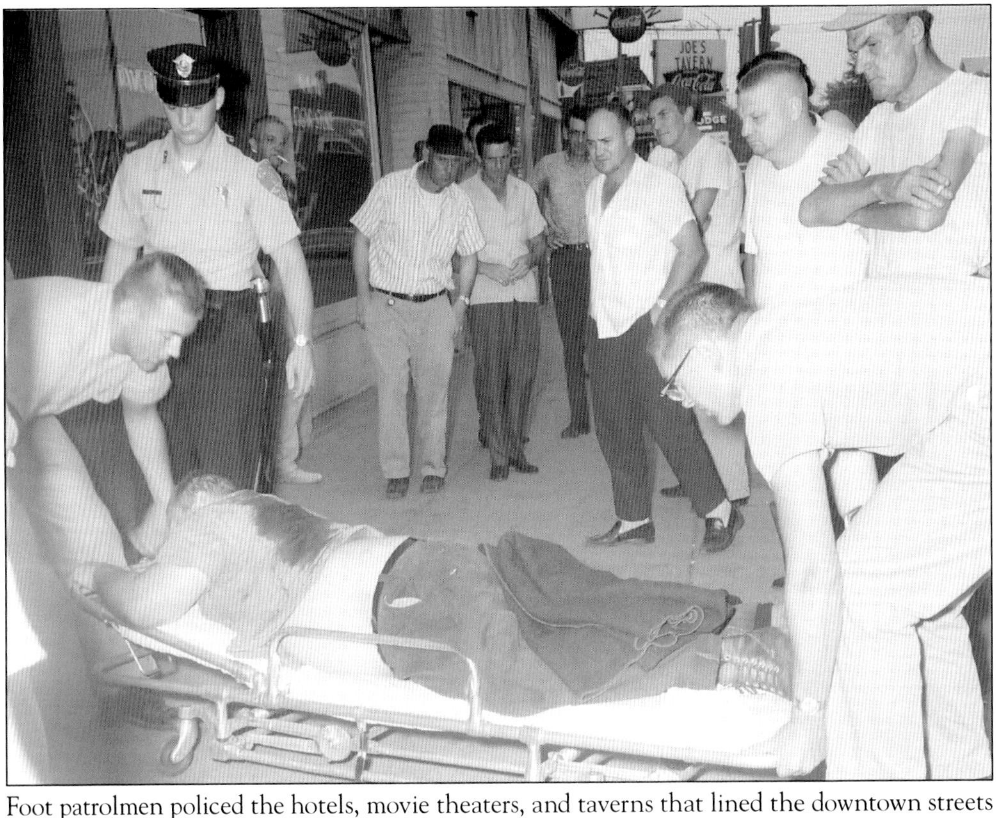

Foot patrolmen policed the hotels, movie theaters, and taverns that lined the downtown streets until the 1970s. It was a tough beat. Here, officer Phil Templin has responded to a stabbing at the Redwood Bar in the 100 block of East Sycamore Street.

Detectives have been called to assist officer Charlie Strasser sort out a tragic accident at North and Morrison Streets. Det. Sgt. Dick Sosbe (wearing glasses) stands in the background at right.

Officer Lynn Rudolph (second from left) has reported for roll call in need of a haircut, to the amusement of Carl Crowder (left), Durwood Whiteman (second from right), and Rodger Fain. The Beatles had recently made their American debut on *The Ed Sullivan Show.* When asked about this photograph, former police chief Rudolph said he was trying to relate to his community.

In 1965, Phil Templin (far left) answered his country's call and, for two years, provided a different level of service—as a soldier. His shift threw him a going-away party in the squad room downtown. Also pictured are, from left to right, Ron Whitacre, Ralph Stroup, Larry Darlin, Barney Maloney, and John Cardwell. Maloney served from 1937 until 1970, when he was forced into retirement at age 65.

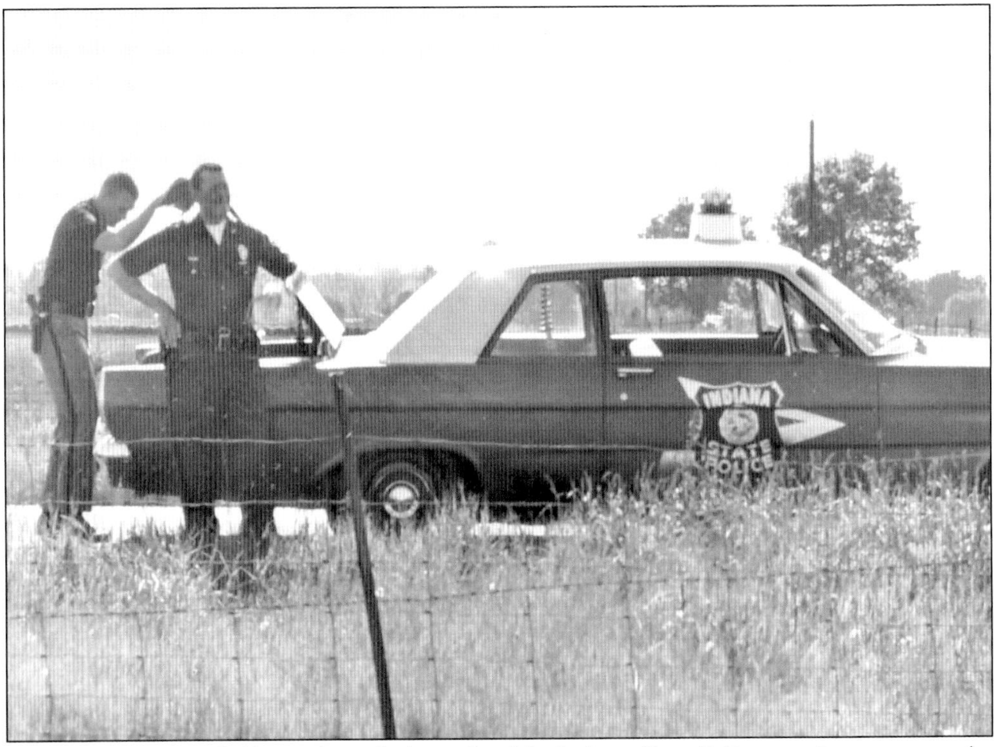

Trooper Jim Goerges (left) rose through the ranks of the Indiana State Police to retire as commander of Peru District in 1992. The merit system for sheriff deputies, enacted into law in 1969, enabled career deputies to further their training and experience, helped to limit politically motivated personnel changes in the Howard County Sheriff's Department, and is one of the most significant changes Goerges saw during his career. Conservation officer Ernie Baker (right) is also pictured.

The jail at 623 South Berkley Road opened in 1964, admitting 12 adult offenders. Facilities were available for 16 women and 5 juveniles in addition to functioning services for patrol operations and living quarters for the sheriff and his family. The living quarters were converted to offices for detectives in 1975 by Sheriff Bob Sargent, and the facility was closed in 1993. Sheriff Tom Leap is pictured.

Kokomo's David Foster Lodge won the Fraternal Order of Police State Basketball Championship in 1964, with a team consisting of troopers and officers. Shown here are, from left to right, (first row) Rex Dillman, Ed Hudson, Bill Kellar, Jake Pickard, and Jack Gabriel; (second row) Andy Castner, Bob Lytle, Max Schroeder, and Bud Cox.

The Kokomo police midnight shift is seen in the squad room of the Walnut Street Station in 1965. Lynn Rudolph (third from left) and watch commander Andy Castner (center, without a hat) would rise through the ranks to lead the department in the next two decades. The lockup, or bum-room, was through the door in the back; the records division was at the window on the right. (Courtesy of Jon Zeck.)

The old jail, constructed in 1893–1894 at 212 South Main Street, had grown obsolete and was razed after Sheriff Tom Leap moved his department into its new home on Berkley Road. Winding steel steps leading to dark and poorly ventilated dungeons absent modern plumbing were no longer considered safe and humane conditions for prisoners. (Courtesy of Elizabeth Kelley Cierzniak.)

Officers Jerry Harrison (left) and Jerry Cody were quick to apprehend the masked gunman who held up a Washington Street dry cleaner. Returned to the scene and instructed to don his mask, the perpetrator was quickly recognized by the victim. Det. Dave Beatty (in glasses next to car) has also arrived at the scene and is organizing the identification.

Officers George Weir (left) and Charlie Strasser (center) pose with Chief Ray Kellar to promote the annual Policeman's Benefit Ball. The event has traditionally raised funds for scholarships and local charities in addition to supporting the Fraternal Order of Police.

The Kokomo Police Department and Howard County Sheriff's Department equipped their patrol cars with two-way radios in 1931. Until portable radios became small enough to be practical, in the early 1970s, dispatchers alerted beat officers downtown that they were needed by activating a series of lights mounted atop downtown buildings. When the lights came on, the beat patrolmen would call the station. Sgt. Spencer Huffman is seen here at the desk. (Courtesy of Jon Zeck.)

Officers Bill Stock (left), Rachel Kirkman, and Larry Darlin pose for a photograph in front of the Walnut Street police station. Assigned as a matron in the Juvenile Aid Division, Kirkman routinely investigated youth-related crimes. Darlin, a graduate of the FBI National Academy, served as assistant chief and chief of police during the progressive 1980s.

A serious accident on Goyer Road prompted a response by the Kokomo Fire Department aerial truck in 1969. Pictured here are, from left to right, officers Ed Hudson, Nate Newsome, and Dick Harrison.

A deputy investigates a rollover accident at Center Road and US 31. Prior to the enactment of vehicle safety standards in the late 1960s, economy vehicles like this Volkswagen offered passengers almost no protection from injury during a crash.

Trooper Darrel Needler (right) crosses the street to investigate a crash in downtown Russiaville. A small group of people, which may include the drivers, chats amicably nearby.

Answering a call for more professional police, the Indiana Legislature created formal qualifications and training requirements for every full-time law enforcement officer in the state. Capt. Bob Sargent developed a local training academy for recruit Howard County deputies and Kokomo police officers. The facilities, which included a gym and an indoor firing range, were located in the city garage, across the street from Kokomo City Hall. (Courtesy of Jay Weir.)

Traffic officers Bob Miller (left), Dick Harrison (center), and Foister Ford pose beside their mounts at the police radio tower on Park Avenue. These officers were responsible for traffic control and meter enforcement in Kokomo's thriving downtown.

A two-hour parking limit ordinance opened parking spaces in Kokomo's bustling downtown. Traffic officers chalked the tires of parked cars and then came back two hours later to make sure they were gone. Scofflaw businessmen had their secretaries move cars around every few hours. Here, officer Bob Miller works his beat at Union and Mulberry Streets.

Officer Ron Beaver (second from left) talks to an unidentified officer at the scene of a fiery car crash near Home Avenue and Hoffer Street. Beaver later distinguished himself as a keen investigator, was seriously injured during a police-action shooting, and became the Kokomo Police Department's first polygraph examiner.

A cross-burning in the summer of 1969 set off several days of rioting and looting in Kokomo's predominately black neighborhoods. In a 12-hour period, 14 policemen, including Kokomo police chief Ray Kellar and state police lieutenant Rex Dillman, were treated for gunshot wounds. The violence erupted near Ned Stahl's produce stand at Monroe Street and North Apperson Way. (Courtesy of Jay Weir.)

During the unrest, Kokomo police were ill prepared for the level of gun violence. Chief Ray Kellar opened a downtown sporting-goods store and emptied the shelves of rifles and ammunition. Prosecutor Fred Osborne raced to Grissom Air Force Base to borrow helmets. Although Kellar had ordered riot training for his officers, Bob Sargent said, "We never had time to get started." State troopers were called to help quell the violence. (Courtesy of Jon Zeck.)

Charlie Hackett was a patrolman during the riots. Many years later, after commanding the SWAT team and then leading the department as chief of police, he said that there was little supplemental training the department could have done to prepare for the violence. "It was guerilla warfare," Hackett said. At the height of the buildup, 200 Indiana state troopers staged from the Kokomo Mall (pictured), Highland Park, and downtown.

Sheriff's deputies often responded to Kokomo police calls for assistance in the city during the turbulent summer and fall of 1969. Prompted by the need for tactical equipment, deputies were issued helmets and were expected to wear them at all times. Here, Capt. Larry Hawks (left) and a helmeted deputy investigate an overturned car.

Snipers fired relentlessly from several houses along Monroe Street. Officers Dick Landis, Jerry Harrison, and Dave Minor were pinned down. Landis had been shot. When their supply of ammunition dwindled, officer Henry Melton tried to reach them with a resupply. He, too, was felled by buckshot. When a tear-gas cartridge set one of the sniper's nests on fire, firefighters were repelled by gunfire from a neighboring house.

Racial tensions flared again after a football game between Kokomo and Lafayette Jefferson in September. A fight broke out in the street near the YMCA, and a black youth was injured while resisting arrest. African Americans blamed police for the violence that followed, and two more officers were wounded by gunfire. Outbreaks of racial violence would rekindle during the next two summers.

The Howard County Civil Defense constructed a headquarters, training facility, and hospital on Berkley Road. During the Cold War, America faced the threat of a nuclear attack by the Soviet Union. Nationwide, the civil defense trained more than 300,000 volunteers in rescue, communications, firefighting, and law enforcement. This facility burned to the ground in 2007. A new structure, operated by the Department of Homeland Security, occupies the site today. (Courtesy of Janice Hart.)

Many innovations came to the Kokomo Police Department in the wake of the race riots of the late 1960s and early 1970s, including a paddy wagon to transport prisoners. The vehicle remained in the fleet through the demise of city court, when it was used to transport prisoners from the jail to Kokomo City Hall. Shown here with the paddy wagon are, from left to right, Ralph Stroup and Chiefs Chuck Sosbe and Ray Kellar.

Troopers referred to their assigned patrol cars as commissions. Throughout the 1960s and 1970s, the cars were replaced when the odometer reached 50,000 miles. This one did not live to retirement. Perhaps this is one of the reasons that officers wear reflective gear when they work in traffic.

Four

The Great Funk
The 1970s

Some people think we just hang a nightstick on a guy and pin a badge on him and that's it. That's an insult to me and the department.

—Lt. Rodger Fain

Like nearly every other American city, Kokomo experienced a dramatic increase in crime during the 1970s. Contributing to a sense of unease were a series of mysterious downtown fires; the Russiaville kidnapping and murders of Connie Fivecoate and her eight-year-old son, Chad; the murder of Steel Inn owner Dorothy Dotterer; the attempted abduction of a woman in broad daylight at the Markland Mall; several police-action shootings; and a host of other, less lethal incidents.

The arbitrary demotion of a captain in 1976 raised concerns about political influences within the Kokomo Police Department, and community leaders began advocating a merit system. Then, two years later, city employees, led by Fraternal Order of Police Lodge 78, participated in an organized work slowdown to protest low wages. After a summer of antics that included blocking traffic with slow-moving patrol cars and driving past Mayor LaDow's house at night with sirens wailing, officers staged an epidemic of 24-hour "blue flu."

The Indiana Law Enforcement Academy began offering mandatory basic training for officers in 1969. But since the Kokomo police already had a training program open to deputies, the first Howard County officers graduated from the IU Bloomington Academy in 1971. The academy moved to its current home in Plainfield in 1975. Several officers in both agencies also took advantage of the Law Enforcement Education Program (LEEP), funded by Congress in 1969 to provide college educations to law enforcement professionals.

Howard County—and the rest of the country for that matter—was asking for a better-trained, better-educated, and more racially and gender-diverse police force. Officers and deputies were equally eager for more training opportunities. They also understood the destructive influence of politics in law enforcement and struggled to keep it at bay, while thumbing their noses at the very people who wrote their paychecks.

Tom Leap (far right) served three terms as sheriff, from 1959 until 1967 and again from 1970 to 1974. The political spoils system that allowed a sheriff to hire and fire his deputies at will had been abolished before Leap started his last term of office, clearing the career path for professional deputies like Ron McGraw (center) and Steve Rogers.

While the number of clandestine groups increased throughout the country in the late 1960s, law enforcement developed intelligence resources to keep track of them. Kokomo police formed a Special Investigations Division (SID) after the 1969 riots and worked closely with state police assets to successfully infiltrate the Indiana Klan. SID evolved into the multijurisdictional Metropolitan Enforcement Group and, later, the Drug Task Force of today. Shown here are Don Howard (left) and Lynn Rudolph.

A Howard County deputy investigates a traffic accident at County Roads 1280 West and 100 South in 1971.

Education and training were seen as means to professionalize law enforcement, and many local officers and deputies were able to enroll in college classes through a federally funded Law Enforcement Education Program (LEEP). Deputy Dick Ferguson and Sheriff Elwood Luellen were among the first local officers to earn degrees through LEEP-assisted tuition programs. Ferguson (pictured) left the sheriff's department in 1972 and retired as a captain from the Kokomo police.

Rachel "Ma" Kirkman joined the Kokomo Police Juvenile Division as a matron in 1950. "Officer" Kirkman wore a police uniform, drove a patrol car, and often made calls involving young offenders. The police department tried unsuccessfully to get her a regular police pension when she left the department in 1971, reasoning that she was doing the same work as the male officers in the Juvenile Aid Division. (Courtesy of Jon Zeck.)

Florence Pogue was hired as Kokomo's first female police officer in 1973. Initially assigned to the juvenile division, she successfully petitioned for a patrol assignment, but nobody could make a decision about her uniform style or what type of calls she would be permitted to handle. Her courage, competence, and determination blazed the trail for all of the women who stand on her shoulders today. (Courtesy of Lynn Rudolph.)

Howard County's first female deputy sheriff, Marty Getz, was appointed in 1973 after testing for a position as an Indiana state trooper. She began her career as a clerk in 1971. Getz is pictured here with Deputy Ted Rose while working as a jail matron. The Indiana State Police did not accept a woman for its recruit school until 1976.

Law enforcement agencies across America worked to cultivate a friendlier, better-educated, better-trained, more culturally diverse and fit image in the 1970s. Police professionalization became the catchphrase of the decade in an attempt to sweep aside the stereotype of the big-bellied, cigar-chewing sheriff. Because female officers were a novelty, Deputy Getz (pictured) could sometimes calm a volatile situation with her mere presence. (Courtesy of Marty Getz.)

During her second year on the job, Getz assisted in the investigation of Connie and Chad Fivecoate's kidnapping and murder. The following year, she worked in an undercover capacity with the Metropolitan Enforcement Group to infiltrate the dangerous Weatherford Family in Lafayette. This resulted in 54 people being indicted on charges ranging from prostitution to drug dealing. She resigned from law enforcement in 1976 after "seeing everything I wanted to see."

A late-night crash at Markland Avenue and Plate Street took out the traffic signals. The police bike in the foreground is a Harley-Davidson Electra Glide with a 58-horsepower engine. It could reach a top speed of 100 miles per hour. Used by the Kokomo police until the early 1980s, these bikes would go for days on five gallons of gasoline.

Greentown marshal Merrill Schrock leads the 1974 Glass Festival Parade through downtown. Along with the annual 4-H Fair, the Glass Festival draws hundreds of people to town each year. The Greentown Special Police was formed to assist the marshal with public events, but it was disbanded after the sheriff revoked its police authority.

The 1974 Greentown Glass Festival provided Marshal Merrill Schrock with an opportunity to test his sharpshooter skills.

Dave Kellar, a third-generation Kokomo policeman, commanded the school liaison program and coordinated several Kokomo Police Department–led juvenile justice initiatives in the late 1980s. He said that "everybody wins anytime a policeman can interact with a kid and bring a positive influence into his life." Officer Henry Melton (left) visits Lyle Mitschelen's driver-training class at Haworth High School in 1975. (Courtesy of Henry Melton.)

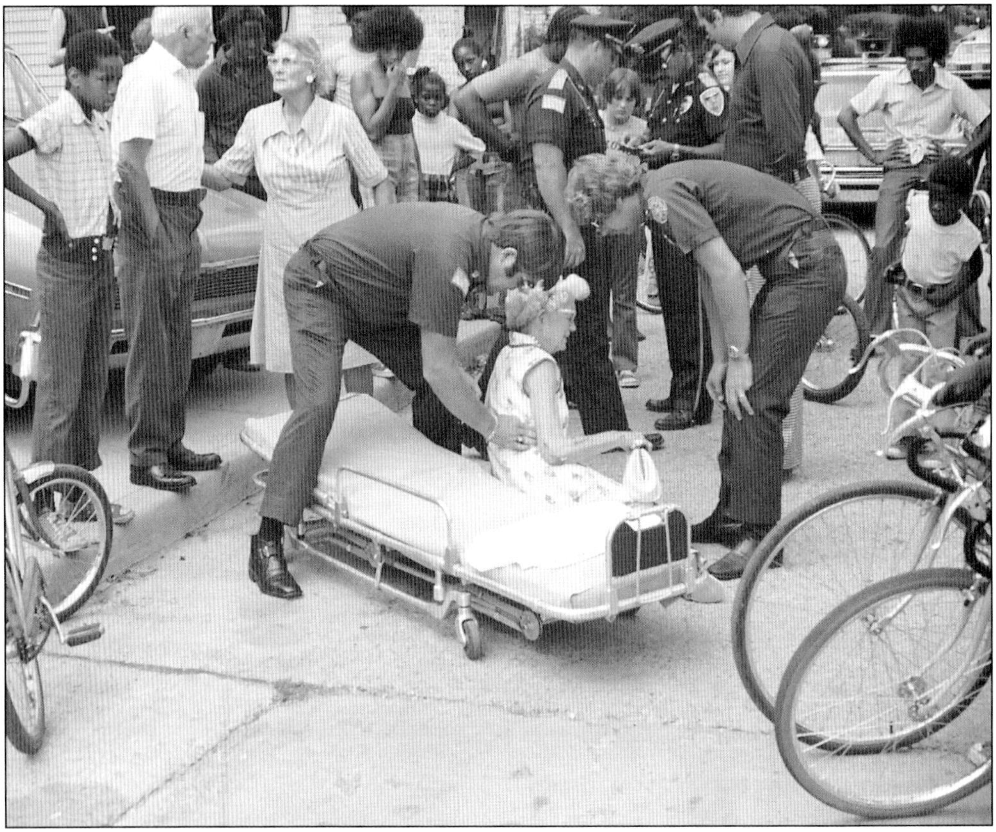

While Kokomo firemen treat a woman who was run down in front of her house, officers Bob Trobaugh and Larry Loveland interview witnesses to try and learn what happened.

Fast, extra-heavy-duty patrol cars were in style before the Middle East oil embargo created an energy crisis that drove police departments to mid-sized sedans. The police and sheriff's departments filled their fleets with these screaming 429-cubic-inch police interceptors. Cooling and transmission problems drove the departments back to more conservative models in 1972. Here, officers Nate Newsome (left) and Jim Catron investigate an accident on Courtland Street in Maple Crest.

Howard County deputy John Beatty (back to the camera) and Burlington town marshal Paul Achor investigate a fatal traffic accident on County Road 1150 West, north of County Road 400 North. A former Indianapolis police officer, then sheriff, Beatty was seriously injured during the 1987 courthouse bombing.

A wrecker was needed to extricate the driver of this Chevy Nova at the Howard County–Miami County line on US 31. Indiana state trooper Jim Miller (foreground) and Kokomo police lieutenant Dick Harrison are helping to get the driver out.

Deputy Jerry Marr was struck by a car while investigating a traffic accident on US 31, south of Center Road. In this photograph, Marr is being readied for hospital transport by Sheriff's Capt. Denny Grishaw (center) and Kokomo Fire Department personnel. An experienced instructor pilot before joining the Howard County Sheriff's Department, Grishaw was instrumental in acquiring the department's first helicopter.

The Hiller 1964 model OH23G helicopter only had 1,300 hours on the meter when Deputies Grishaw, Roger Smith, and Jim Scales acquired the aircraft through a Civil Defense–US Army surplus acquisition program in 1974. To facilitate and lower pilot training costs, Grishaw talked the National Guard out of a set of dual controls for the two-seat helicopter. (Courtesy of Marty Getz.)

Although the helicopter burned 18 gallons of high-octane aviation gasoline every hour, at 50¢ per gallon, it proved to be an economical investment. Initially, insurance premiums only totaled $275 a year, while the sheriff's department used its aircraft to search for missing children and to rescue stranded motorists, as during a 1976 blizzard (pictured). The helicopter would serve 1,200 hours in the air before being retired in 1983. (Courtesy of Marty Getz.)

"Little Dusty" became useful in monitoring traffic during public events and as a photography platform for investigative purposes. But costs were rising. By 1981, insurance was eating away at the operating budget, and the sheriff's department could afford only about 11 hours of flight time per year. Deputy Steve Maus, who learned how to fly through the sheriff's department, is seen here behind the controls.

Kokomo police have responded to a traffic accident at Union and Walnut Streets. Most of the downtown streets were designated for one-way travel in the 1950s to provide for an orderly flow of traffic in the event of a nuclear attack, and they remained that way until long after the Cold War was over. The dark sedan on the right is a Kokomo Fire Department vehicle.

Deputy Mark Fisher mans the radio and answers phones at the Berkley Road Jail in 1975. Electrical storms would sometimes send a shocking electrical charge through the microphone and to the lips of anybody who was broadcasting. It would be two decades before city and county dispatchers worked under the same roof.

Haworth High School established the first local organization for youth who were interested in law enforcement careers—the Law Enforcement Club. Since club members helped patrol the parking lots and hallways, they came to be dubbed the "Haworth Police Department" by other students, and club members wore caps bearing the acronym HPD. Police liaison officer and faculty advisor Sgt. Joe Click hosted the program, which included 13 senior men and women during the 1973–1974 school year. For reasons unknown, the HPD was not recognized by Haworth's Club Council after the charter group graduated. (1974 Haworth *Subracus*.)

HPD's Engine No. 1 comes to the rescue! Haworth seniors Steve Baldwin (left) and John Groves help other students get out of the parking lot in the middle of a December 19, 1973, blizzard that closed school for the year. The 1966 Volkswagen van, not an official vehicle by any means, was reputed to keep going even in the toughest terrain. (1974 Haworth *Subracus*.)

Haworth principal Harry McCool endorsed the HPD as a police career introduction program. But, other than to allow school liaison officer Sgt. Bill Click to act as faculty advisor, the Kokomo police refused to have anything to do with the youth program. Here, HPD members Susan Brown and Ed Rutherford patrol the Haworth parking lots. At least three former HPD members entered police careers, including Jack Rosa, who became a US marshal.

People who knew Deputy Jerry Marr, seen here at a sheriff's tent during the Howard County 4-H Fair, will remember his commitment to youth, his attention to the image of professional deputies, and particularly his outstanding leadership in the aftermath of the tragic courthouse bombing 10 years after this photograph was taken. It is unfortunate that his legacy was tarnished in the next century.

Recruit officers, deputies, and troopers were formally initiated into the David Foster Lodge of the Fraternal Order of Police at the conclusion of their respective probationary periods. The initiation was considered a rite of passage, but the practice was discontinued when the tradition of hazing employees became taboo.

Dietra Jackson became Kokomo's first black female officer in 1974. She felt that Flo Pogue, who had been hired a year earlier, had "broken the ice" for female officers. Unlike Pogue, who believed that she was under constant scrutiny because of her gender, Jackson tried not to compete with her male counterparts and tailored the job to her own unique and often feminine style. (Courtesy of the *Kokomo Tribune*.)

Citizens were sometimes surprised to find a woman behind the badge, but Dietra Jackson will not admit to having faced prejudice from the black community for her career choice. In a 1982 interview with the *Kokomo Tribune*, Jackson said, "I have 107 brothers and a sister," and they are all blue. Dietra Jackson retired as a detective in 1994. (Courtesy of the *Kokomo Tribune*.)

Law Enforcement Explorer Post 2599 was sponsored by the Howard County Sheriff's Department in 1975. Organized by Deputy Jerry Marr under the initiative of Sheriff Bob Sargent, the program was affiliated with the Boy Scouts of America to introduce young men and women to careers in law enforcement. Many of these explorers, like Jerry Williams (on the telephone) became police officers, deputies, or troopers.

Howard County Law Enforcement Explorers relax with advisor Bill Bean (third from left) in the jail kitchen. Also pictured are, from left to right, Kathy Muhl, unidentified, Teresa Kaufman, Jerry Williams, and Tammy Pearson. Before an explorer could accompany a road deputy on patrol, they were required to complete a training program that included working around the jail in a variety of service and operational capacities.

Kokomo policemen named in suit

LAFAYETTE, Ind. — Three Kokomo policemen have been named defendants in a $10,000 damage suit filed here on behalf of a woman who contends she was not paid for all of her work in making drug buys.

According to the civil complaint in Tippecanoe Circuit Court, Karen Smith, formerly of Kokomo and now of Lafayette, was used by the officers as a go-between to arrange buys from illegal drug dealers so arrests could be made.

Defendants listed in the action are John Hurlock, John Ashenfelter and Lynn Rudolph.

The plaintiff's attorney is Lewis T. Wireman who has been indicted by a grand jury here on 12 burglary and theft-related counts. He is a former Lafayette city court judge.

The plaintiff alleges she was a Kokomo resident when she began working for the policemen, but continued work for them after moving to Lafayette. Some of the persons with whom she set up buys were later indicted by the grand jury.

She contends in the suit that because police do not have legal authority to operate in Tippecanoe County, she may be subject to arrest resulting from her contact with illegal drug dealers.

Hurlock and Rudolph were or are officers assigned to a 14-county special investigation division headquartered here, and a Gary Ashenfelter has been with the unit.

The $10,000 is asked to cover legal costs if the plaintiff woman is arrested and to pay for about $300 she claims is owed her by the police.

Officers of the Howard County–based Metropolitan Enforcement Group stirred up a hornet's nest of corruption in Tippecanoe County during a 1975 drug investigation. Among those indicted was a former city court judge, who had orchestrated a burglary resulting in the theft of guns. A total of 54 indictments were handed down, resulting in the arrest of 16 people and implicating the Lafayette police and the Tippecanoe County prosecutor's office. A subsequent FBI wiretap revealed that Sara Roberts, the mother of a Lafayette policeman and secretary in the US Probation and Parole Service, was leaking information to Michael Weatherford, the principal target of the investigation. An FBI probe ran into 1982, when federal judge Allen Sharp, who was estranged from his wife and dating Roberts, interceded on her behalf. After the US attorney decided not to prosecute Roberts, Judge Sharp accused the FBI of harassment in a letter to FBI director William Webster. Weatherford remained a fugitive until 1983, when he was arrested in Florida. He was subsequently sentenced to life imprisonment. (Courtesy of Marty Getz.)

The Police Athletic League (PAL) was formed when the Kokomo YMCA stopped funding its intramural football program. Officer Gene Wingate organized the program, which was turned over to Sgt. "Robbie" Robertson in 1980. Robertson, seen here issuing uniforms, solicited the funding that allowed for a sports facility and inclusion of various other athletic opportunities. PAL's goal is to build character by providing civic and athletic opportunities to community youth. (Courtesy of Lynn Rudolph.)

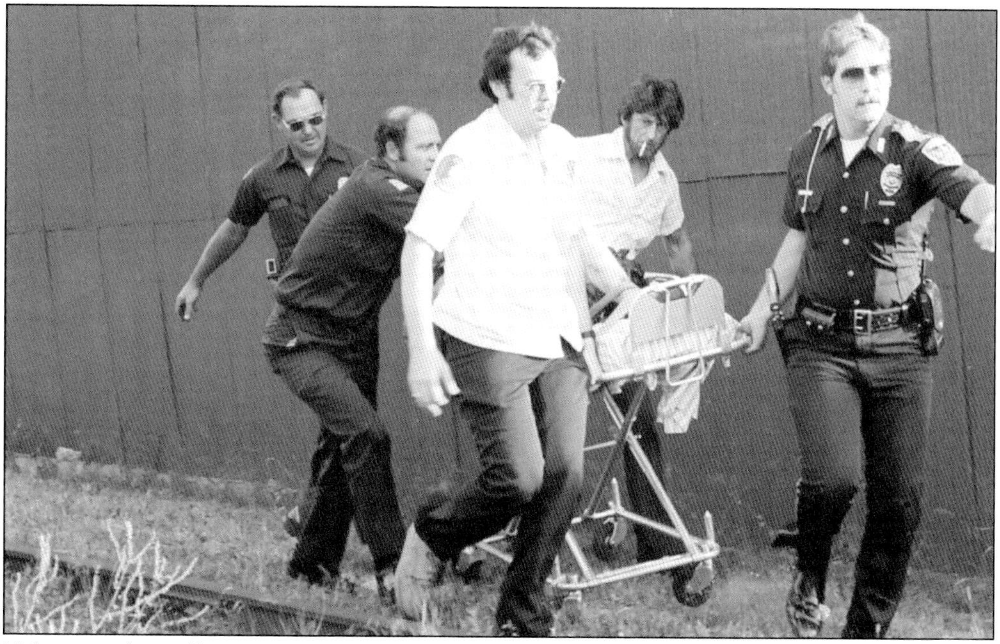

Kokomo police officers were expected by policy to wear their uniform hats anytime they were outdoors. So, when somebody ran off the end of Buckeye Street into Wildcat Creek, and officer Gary Guest helped firefighters pull him to safety bare-headed, the police chief wanted him reprimanded. Punishment was avoided after Guest's superiors interceded on his behalf. A new uniform policy in 1980 banished the hat as well as neckties for all, except as part of the formal dress uniform.

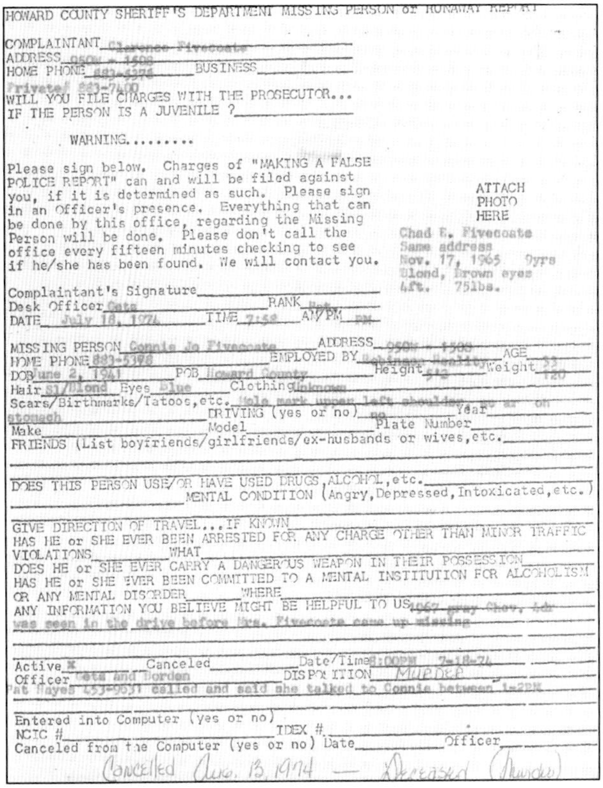

HOWARD COUNTY SHERIFF'S DEPARTMENT MISSING PERSON or RUNAWAY REPORT

COMPLAINANT Clarence Fivecoate
ADDRESS 050W - 1500
HOME PHONE 883-4376 BUSINESS
Private# 883-7400
WILL YOU FILE CHARGES WITH THE PROSECUTOR...
IF THE PERSON IS A JUVENILE ?

WARNING........

Please sign below. Charges of "MAKING A FALSE POLICE REPORT" can and will be filed against you, if it is determined as such. Please sign in an Officer's presence. Everything that can be done by this office, regarding the Missing Person will be done. Please don't call the office every fifteen minutes checking to see if he/she has been found. We will contact you.

ATTACH PHOTO HERE

Chad E. Fivecoate
Same address
Nov. 17, 1965 9yrs
Blond, Brown eyes
4ft. 75lbs.

Complainant's Signature
Desk Officer Getz RANK Sgt.
DATE July 18, 1974 TIME 7:50 AM/PM pm

MISSING PERSON Connie Jo Fivecoate ADDRESS 050W - 1500
HOME PHONE 883-5398 EMPLOYED BY Robinson Realty AGE 33
DOB June 2, 1941 POB Howard County Height 5'2 Weight 120
Hair Sl/Blond Eyes Blue Clothing Unknown
Scars/Birthmarks/Tatoos,etc. Mole mark upper left shoulder, scar on stomach DRIVING (yes or no) no Year
Make Model Plate Number
FRIENDS (List boyfriends/girlfriends/ex-husbands or wives,etc.

DOES THIS PERSON USE/OR HAVE USED DRUGS,ALCOHOL,etc.
MENTAL CONDITION (Angry,Depressed,Intoxicated,etc.)

GIVE DIRECTION OF TRAVEL...IF KNOWN
HAS HE or SHE EVER BEEN ARRESTED FOR ANY CHARGE OTHER THAN MINOR TRAFFIC VIOLATIONS WHAT
DOES HE or SHE EVER CARRY A DANGEROUS WEAPON IN THEIR POSSESSION
HAS HE or SHE EVER BEEN COMMITTED TO A MENTAL INSTITUTION FOR ALCOHOLISM OR ANY MENTAL DISORDER WHERE
ANY INFORMATION YOU BELIEVE MIGHT BE HELPFUL TO US 1967 gray Chev. 4dr was seen in the drive before Mrs. Fivecoate came up missing

Active X Canceled Date/Time 8:00PM 7-18-74
Officer Getz and Borden DISPOSITION MURDER
Pat Hayes 453-9631 called and said she talked to Connie between 1-2PM

Entered into Computer (yes or no)
NCIC # IDEX #
Canceled from the Computer (yes or no) Date Officer
Cancelled Aug. 13, 1974 — Deceased (Murder)

Deputy Marty Getz took the initial missing-persons report when the wife and son of a prominent Kokomo businessman disappeared from their Russiaville home in 1974. Even before Connie Fivecoate's car was discovered abandoned in Huston Park, Getz feared that the family had met with violence. Charles Lockert, an accomplice in the kidnapping, rape, and double murder, would later lead sheriff's detectives to the bodies. (Courtesy of Marty Getz.)

Indiana State Police detective Darrel Needler found blood traces and a strand of long blond hair, believed to have come from Connie Fivecoate, in Ralph Murphy's Ford Galaxie. The bodies of Connie and her eight-year-old son, Chad, had been discovered near Monterey in Starke County. Needler is in the center of this photograph, taken in the Berkley Road Jail. The number in the center of the status board on the wall represents total inmates.

EDITORIALS

4 KOKOMO (Ind.) TRIBUNE Saturday, Oct. 23, 1976

A captain's demotion

The demotion of Capt.Phil Templin of the Kokomo Police Department has raised some serious questions, the first of which is: What is the reason for the demotion?

According to Police Chief Keith Anderson and Mayor Arthur LaDow, the step was taken by the city administration because of "morale problems" in the police department. Whether or not this is the real reason, the sequence of events in the span of eight days can lead any reasonable reader to conclude that Templin was "busted" because he exercised his right of free speech.

Here is what happened: A reader's letter was published in The Tribune on Tuesday, Oct.12. Signed by "D.E.R.," it was critical of speeding on South Washington Street and sought to put the blame on alleged lax police patrolling.

Capt.Templin considered the letter to be unfair criticism of policemen and wrote in reply. Published Friday, Oct.15, his letter defended the police and mentioned that they are unfairly under attack from chronic complainers. He inserted one general paragraph as follows: "We (police) wonder if it is really worth all the hassle we take from the people, the administration, prosecutors and courts. It seems as though we have very little support."

On Monday, Oct.18, Templin was called to Mayor LaDow's office where, Templin says, the Mayor expressed a feeling that Templin's remarks about "the administration" were directed to the Mayor personally and to his administration. Templin says his choice of the term "administration" was directed to all who have part in the control of police affairs. This would include not only the Mayor and Board of Public Works, but the city council as well. Yet a question must be asked: Did the present "city administration" take it as derogatory to itself and was Templin punished for saying what he did the way he said it?

At any rate, on Wednesday, Oct.20, Templin was called into Chief Anderson's office and was told he was being relieved of his command on Friday, Oct.22. The action must be authorized by the board of works next Monday before becoming official.

If Templin was demoted for what he wrote, it is a petty kind of discipline, reflecting an unseemly sensitivity on the administration's part. He is a citizen and has a right to speak his views as has any other citizen. How can any organization expect to become aware of any problems needing attention if its members are under fear of some type of discipline if they open their mouths?

Was the reason for 'busting officer the fact that he exercised right of free speech in letter?

Templin's main purpose in his letter was to defend the police, an organization to which he has devoted 13 years of his life as well as many off-duty hours for college study to improve his abilities as a policeman. In the course of doing so he decried what he said was a lack of cooperation from the public and from officials. The language "D.E.R." used in his letter criticizing the police (such phrases as "tin-badge heroes") was enough to stir resentment among the city's policemen, and it was not unnatural that Templin would respond to it forcefully. His criticism of "D.E.R.'s" letter was well taken.

Surely the police chief, Mayor LaDow and the Board of Public Works must have considered how the public would consider the demotion of a police captain in view of the series of events of the past several days. One must regard the demotion as a "reminder" to police that they can't speak out like other citizens, or those who determined the demotion must have a massive packet of specific evidence to prove that Capt. Templin is largely responsible for any and all morale problems the police department may have.

It seems to us that come Monday, when presumably the Templin case will be discus[illegible] the board of works meet there needs to be presented substantial documented proof that the demotion was done in the best interests of the police department and the community and not in reaction to Templin exercising his right to express his views. Any cursory action by the board of works will be considered by the community as an admission that Templin is the object of a petty action.

A second, and most urgent question arises from this incident: When will a nonpartisan citizens committee be named to study the feasibility and desirability of instituting a merit system for the police and fire departments?

Under the existing political system, in which policemen are promoted or demoted according to the wishes of whatever administration is in office, men finding themselves chastised as Templin seems to have been have little, if any, recourse. If Kokomo had a merit system, these men would have a place, possibly a nonpartisan merit board, where they could be assured they would get a full and fair hearing before being thrown into the outdated political yo-yo system of demotion, promotion and lateral transfers.

A workable merit system has been found by a number of communities around the nation where police and firefighters are rated on the basis of their professional abilities and talents and not on their politics. We believe such a system can be created here.But first, as we have advocated several times before, there is a need for a nonpartisan committee to be set up to study the matter. A committee of citizens who have personnel management and administrative skills as well as knowledge of the police and fire department functions should be named forthwith.

This should become a top-priority item for the city administration.

Captain Templin's demotion brought public focus to political corruption within the Kokomo Police Department. Chief Keith Anderson resigned for the "good of the department," and a citizens' "Blue Ribbon Committee" was formed to study the benefits of a civilian merit board to oversee police department personnel matters. It would be four more years before Chief Rodger Fain established a policy that discouraged political manipulation of his department. (Courtesy of the *Kokomo Tribune*.)

Capt. Phil Templin (far right), pictured in 1986 when he was captain of detectives, found himself surrounded in controversy 10 years earlier after offending Mayor Art LaDow in a letter to the editor of the *Kokomo Tribune*. Templin's demotion sparked a public outcry for the elimination of politics in the Kokomo police. On the left in this photograph is Lt. John Hurlock, commanding the burglary/robbery section.

The Howard County Civil Defense, forerunner to the Emergency Management Agency, historically enjoyed a close working relationship with the police and sheriff's departments. Here, a civil defense patrol car is included in a law enforcement display at the Kokomo Mall. (Courtesy of Janice Hart.)

Low wages contributed to morale problems among all City of Kokomo employees in 1978. At the height of wage negotiations with the Fraternal Order of Police, officers staged a series of job actions, including a slowdown, an epidemic of "blue flu," and the picketing of city hall. (Courtesy of Jay Weir.)

The combination of a politically powerful mayor and weak leadership in the police department had resulted in a breakdown in command and eroding pay and benefits, as well as rundown facilities, training, and equipment. Bob Trobaugh (right) and the FOP led a protest and slowdown, followed by a complete work stoppage. The events, according to Chief Andy Castner, brought cohesion back to the ranks and restored the morale of the police department. Also pictured in this 1981 image are Art Fross (foreground) and Michael Holsapple. (Courtesy of Kokomo Police Department.)

Howard County sheriff's detectives Lee Eckert (left) and Herb Becraft (center) assist Deputy John Beaty at an accident scene on US 35. By the end of the decade, city, county, and state police sent selected officers to Northwestern University for specialized training in traffic-accident investigation.

Det. Sgt. John Cardwell was recognized nationally after he led two Kokomo police vehicle-theft investigations. Using carefully recruited operatives, Cardwell (pictured) infiltrated a stolen-car-parts ring (chop shop) operating out of Toledo, and an interstate truck-hijacking ring. Lynn Rudolph, who headed the detective division at that time, said that the investigations were probably as close as the Kokomo police ever got to the Mafia. (Courtesy of the *Kokomo Tribune*.)

While Jeffery Hand was abducting a woman from the parking lot outside Sears, Deputy Sheriff Vernal Baugh (pictured) was off duty, shopping with his wife on the other side of Markland Mall. Over his police radio, he heard Kokomo police send a patrol car to investigate the commotion at Sears. Baugh pulled up on the south side of the mall in time to see the suspect fleeing from the parking lot with his victim.

A brief chase ensued, and Hand lost control of his car in a snowdrift and bailed out, leaving his intended victim behind. Hand tried to run, but Baugh chased him with his police car. When the opportunity presented itself, Baugh jumped out and knocked the suspect down. Baugh began walking Hand back to the police car at gunpoint. (Courtesy of the *Kokomo Tribune*.)

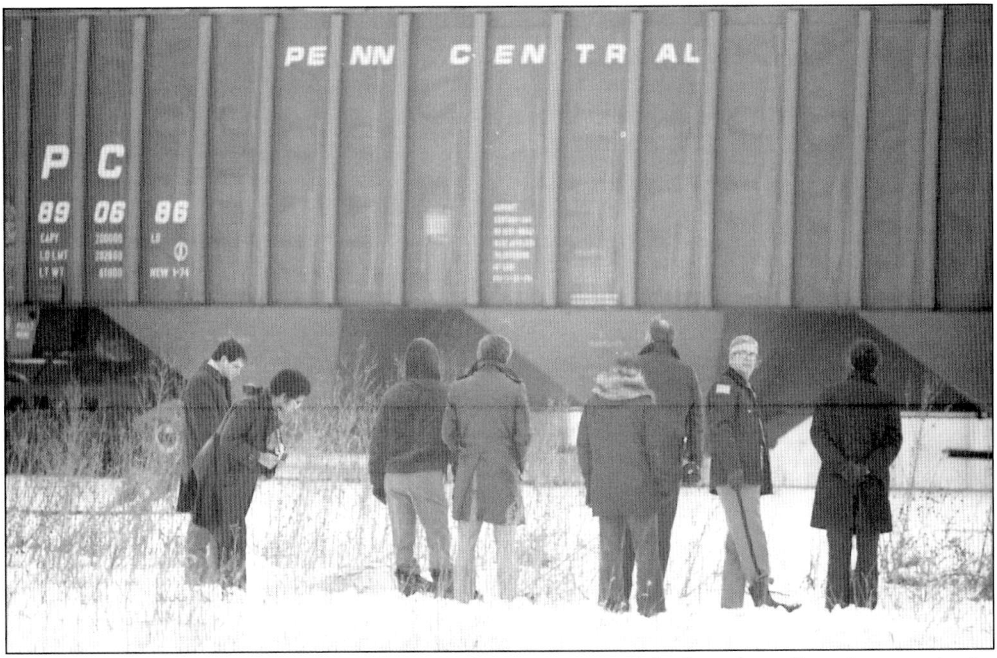

Deputy Baugh was unaware that Jeffery Hand was a man with little to lose. Found not guilty by reason of insanity in a Vigo County murder, Hand had escaped from a mental institution. While Baugh used his radio to ask for assistance, Hand spun around and shot him. An exchange of gunfire ensued as Hand made yet another escape. (Courtesy of the *Kokomo Tribune*.)

Kokomo police officer Jerry Kassel arrived in time to see the gun battle and thought that Baugh had been killed. Then, he spotted Hand running into the field at the dead end of Seventeenth Street and gave chase. As Hand reached a set of railroad tracks and kept running, Kassel ordered him to stop. Hand kept going. Again, Kassel ordered him to stop. (Courtesy of the *Kokomo Tribune*.)

Jeffery Hand had abducted a young woman from a busy parking lot in broad daylight. He had shot and seriously wounded a deputy sheriff while escaping from custody. He was armed and running along the tracks near busy US 31. When Officer Kassel's second order to stop was ignored, Hand died of a single gunshot wound. Just four minutes had elapsed since the initial dispatch was broadcast. (Courtesy of the *Kokomo Tribune*.)

Officers Bob Reynolds and Jerry Kassel investigate a serious accident in front of the Brada-Miller Freight Terminal at Virginia Avenue and Apperson Way. Motorcycle officers, in helmets, britches, and boots, rode both two- and three-wheel machines, depending on their assignments. Due to their maneuverability, the motorcycles were very useful for traffic enforcement and crowd control.

Mandy Lewellen's body was discovered, 11 days after she disappeared, in woods near Northwestern Schools. Detectives quickly learned that Bobby Avery, who was free on bond while waiting to be sentenced for rape, was making plans to leave for Arkansas. In this photograph, police and sheriff deputies swarm the crime scene. John Hurlock is seen right of center, pointing.

Since Mandy Lewellen lived in the city, but was last seen in the county, Kokomo police detectives worked closely with sheriff's deputies throughout the course of the investigation. Deputy Steve Rogers (pointing) and Det. Mark Thompson locate an item of evidence near the body, while other investigators examine the surrounding areas. (Courtesy of the *Kokomo Tribune*.)

Deputy prosecuting attorney Dennis Parry (center) arrived at the grisly scene to be briefed and to provide legal advice. Bobby Avery would later receive a 40-year sentence. The Honorable Dennis Parry served several terms as judge of Howard Superior Court. (Courtesy of the *Kokomo Tribune*.)

Lt. John Hurlock (left) consults Sgts. Tom Melton (center) and Don Mills outside the woods where Mandy Lewellen's body was discovered. Over the next several weeks, these detectives recruited two of Avery's friends to record statements he made about fleeing Indiana. A bond revocation was requested, allowing detectives to pick up Avery for questioning. Sheriff Bob Sargent is on the far right in this photograph. (Courtesy of the *Kokomo Tribune*.)

Kokomo police were able to put more officers on the street when dispatch services moved into the new fire department headquarters. Civilian telecommunications operators Becky Kidwell (background on left) and Jeanette Huffman (right) fielded 9-1-1 emergency calls, coordinated street-patrol operations, and linked local officers with the National Crime Information Center. Dispatchers were required to ride along on patrols for training purposes during their assigned shifts.

Lt. Paul Reed has taken a man into custody after he set fire to a house near West Markland and Millbrook Avenues. The arsonist had been captured by some civic-minded youths who held the man until police arrived. The once proud Continental Steel Mill stands in the background of this photograph.

People call the police when they have a problem and do not know where to go for help. By the late 1970s, less than 15 percent of an officer's or deputy's time was spent dealing with criminals or criminal matters. Here, Deputy Steve Rogers cautiously makes friends with a stray dog. (Courtesy of the *Kokomo Tribune*.)

Indiana state troopers Jeff Stinson (left) and Bob Lather proudly represent the Peru District during the funeral of retired Kokomo police officer Les Sosbe. The Peru Post, formerly identified as District 23 and based along a lonely stretch of Business US 31 north of Peru, was an integral part of the Howard County law enforcement family. Lather was killed in the line of duty three years after this photograph was taken.

A nationwide increase in armed confrontations with police created interest in training and equipping small tactical units. Here, the Kokomo police SWAT team practices with the Air Force Security Police at Grissom Air Force Base. Pictured here are, from left to right, officers Roger Schwartz, Norris Jones, Gary Conwell, and Charlie Hackett. The Howard County Sheriff's Department and the Indiana State Police trained their own teams. (Courtesy of Norris Jones.)

Sheriff's deputies and Greentown marshals investigate a traffic accident on State Road 35, east of Greentown. The Greentown marshal and his deputies train with the Howard County Sheriff's Department, and the two agencies complement one another to provide eastern Howard County with a quality of public safety neither agency could deliver by itself.

Five

Pudding Pops to Briefcase Bombs
The 1980s

The cops and the Klan go hand in hand.

—Communist Workers Party chant during 1980 KKK march

City officials were uneasy when the Ku Klux Klan asked for a permit to march through the streets of downtown Kokomo. The request came on the heels of a tragedy in Greensboro, North Carolina, in which five counterdemonstrators had been murdered by Klansmen during a similar event. Refusing to grant the permit did not appear to be an option, so newly elected mayor Steve Daily turned to his new police chief, with instructions to keep the community safe.

The whole country was watching in April 1980 when the parading Klansmen were quietly slipped into an alley in the back of a rental truck, pushed into a forced march around the courthouse by three squads of highly trained and disciplined crowd-control teams, and then routed back to their waiting truck. This all took place under the menacing stares of riot-trained state troopers, who had filed out of the courthouse and lined the sidewalks. The tactics devised by Howard County law enforcement became a template for the response to similar events around the county.

The 1980s also ushered in a new era for Howard County law enforcement. As soon as the Klan march was over, Chief Rodger Fain set about raising the bar for the Kokomo police. Surrounded by veteran officers who shared his vision, he put in place higher standards for the recruitment and selection of new officers, mandatory fitness requirements were established, and a budget was made available to help officers with college tuition. The training division not only scheduled and provided specialized instruction, but also carefully examined officer-involved shootings, traffic accidents, and use-of-force complaints before visiting roll calls, to explain how the job could be done better.

And, for the first time, supervisors and commanders were held accountable for the efficiency and professionalism of their subordinates, thus creating a clear chain of command and improving the effectiveness of the department.

Just five months after the deadly Greensboro massacre, the Ku Klux Klan staged a parade on the streets of downtown Kokomo. While city, county, and state police commanders developed a plan, joint police and sheriff's riot teams trained together. Undercover officers began following Klan and counter-Klan activities, and detectives sought recommendations from other communities where Klan events had resulted in violence.

Klan members were trucked downtown by police and surrounded by a protective wedge of policemen and deputies. Then, 10 minutes before the march was advertised to begin, the wedge of lawmen walked the Klansmen quickly around the courthouse. Indiana state troopers dressed in full riot gear emerged from the courthouse and lined the sidewalks bordering the march.

Marchers had nearly returned to their starting point at an alley in the 100 block of West Sycamore Street and had told their escorts that they intended to go around again when they were met by counterdemonstrators at Sycamore and Main Streets. The idea was ignored by police, who walked them back into the alley and loaded the robed and masked Klansmen into a waiting U-Haul truck.

The sheriff's riot team had been at the very back of the wedge that protected the Klansmen. When the marchers were safely aboard their rescue vehicle, the deputies turned to confront members of the Communist Workers Party. These marchers, who had followed the parade to the alley, were wearing helmets and holding two-inch-by-two-inch boards that had supported their signs.

Police threatened the counterdemonstrators with tear gas when they refused to disperse, and, after 30 minutes, they evaporated into the afternoon. Local police handling of the incident was heralded nationwide as a template for similar events and was copied around the country. The only glitch occurred when somebody opened Sycamore Street to traffic and introduced terrified motorists to the rage of the crowd.

Trooper Bob Lather had just pulled off a prowler call near Bunker Hill on July 6, 1982, when he learned that Howard County deputies were chasing a suspect northbound on US 31. Lather initiated a "rolling roadblock" tactic in an attempt to slow or stop the offender. He was killed when the suspect's vehicle collided with his patrol car. (Courtesy of Indiana State Police.)

An eight-year veteran of the Indiana State Police, Bob Lather was assigned to Peru District, with principal responsibility for Howard County. He had lived in Greentown. Since the state police and the sheriff's department did not share a common radio frequency, deputies were unaware of Lather's efforts to assist until after the tragic crash. (Courtesy of Indiana State Police.)

Don "Ducky" and Betty Duncan, owners of Ducky's Restaurant on East Markland Avenue, were friends of law enforcement for many years. Ducky would often show up at the police station with a pot of chili and a box of sandwiches during holidays, when most restaurants were closed. Citizens, and even the media on occasion, were critical of the city, county, and state police cars that crowded Ducky's parking lot. (Courtesy of the *Kokomo Tribune*.)

Deputies Jon Zeck (foreground) and Tim Martin (background) investigate a rear-end collision in the southbound traffic lanes of US 31 and State Road 26. Deputy prosecutor Michael Krebs (in sunglasses), who was riding with Zeck, is also pictured.

Detectives were expected to know everything: who did what to whom, when they did it, and who married his sister. That all changed with computer technology, which made it possible to store and retrieve vast amounts of data about crime, suspects, stolen property, and even criminal intelligence. Here, Dave Andrews works with an early desktop. It would be 10 more years before the technology made the detectives' work any easier. (Courtesy of Lynn Rudolph.)

Peter Maris organized a "terror squad" attack against Kokomo for his low-budget movie of the same name. Known mostly for poor production quality and blundering characters, *Terror Squad* stars Chuck Connors, of television's *The Rifleman*, and Brodie Greer, of *CHiPs* fame. The 1988 film features a spectacular car chase through downtown Kokomo. This crash was filmed in Highland Park. (Kokomo Police Department.)

Lt. John Brown (right), dressed here for his role as an extra in *Terror Squad*, worked closely with Maris and Connors during filming in Kokomo. The community's hospitality to the filmmaker included using local people, including policemen, as extras. Filming is taking place at Buckeye and Mulberry Streets in front of the once very popular China Clipper Chow Mein Restaurant. Capt. "Robbie" Robertson is also pictured. (Courtesy of Lynn Rudolph.)

Urban policing is statistically more dangerous than rural law enforcement, even though Kokomo police officers work in an environment where help is usually a block away. Troopers and deputies, on the other hand, often work alone and far from the reinforcement of a nearby backup officer. Here, deputy Don Leffert administers a field sobriety test on a lonely stretch of county blacktop.

Officer Don Bolan directs traffic after a signal malfunctioned along Jefferson Street. Typically, some drivers are better at taking direction than others, as reflected in Bolan's face. (Courtesy of the *Kokomo Tribune*.)

Budget limitations and rising fuel costs prompted Sheriff Bob Sargent to put his administrative deputies in compact, gas-sipping police cars. School liaison Deputy Don Howard (pictured) drew the attention of students when he stuck a scale windup key on the back of his Chevy Citation. The little cars did not last long under the crushing demands of law enforcement service and were replaced by grown-up police cars.

Howard County Civil Defense, the forerunner of the Emergency Management Agency and now the Department of Homeland Security, was comprised of fire, rescue, communications, and police components. Volunteers could serve Howard County in a manner that was best suited to their skills and interests. Here, a civil defense officer blocks traffic at Superior and Main Streets during the Haynes-Apperson Festival. (Courtesy of Janice Hart.)

In the background of this scene behind North Lafountain Street, Jim Smith is telling detectives how Ballard White got shot over a pair of shoes. It all began on East Mulberry Street, when White took a shot at another man with a pistol and got his pickup truck riddled with a shotgun blast. Dave Kellar (far left) and the author (back to camera) are also pictured. (Courtesy of the *Kokomo Tribune*.)

Tom Dinardo (second from left) assists John Hurlock (center) with the investigation behind the 1500 block of North Lafountain Street, while Capt. Dick Sosbe (second from right) confers with Asst. Chief Larry Darlin. It was here that Ballard White met up again with the guy who shot up his truck. Again, White fired his pistol, and, again, somebody called the police. White was sitting in his truck when officers Art Fross and Jim Smith arrived. (Courtesy of the *Kokomo Tribune.*)

The officers approached Ballard White from behind, spreading out, with Art Fross on the driver's side and Jim Smith on the other. White saw them coming and rolled through the open truck door to get a shot off at Fross. As he sat back up in the cab, Fross returned fire. White survived his wound. Here, officers have responded to the "shots fired" radio call and seek cover before the scene is secured. (Courtesy of the *Kokomo Tribune.*)

A vehicle pursuit ended north of Kokomo, when the suspects cut across somebody's backyard and crashed into a house. Officer Gary Guest chased the driver south, while the passenger, pursued by the author, ran around the corner of this house and waited in ambush. Guest shot him in the back with a shotgun as the suspect raised a pistol to the author's head. (Courtesy of the *Kokomo Tribune.*)

Officer Gary Guest went back to look for the driver while backup units from the city and county converged on the rural neighborhood along Road 150 West. Guest was briefly pinned down after the driver forced his way into a house and started shooting at officers from an upstairs window. Officer Bob Beeler, using a moving patrol car for cover, was able to rescue Guest from the line of fire. (Courtesy of the *Kokomo Tribune.*)

Gary Ashenfelter (left) and another detective dive for cover while Kokomo police SWAT members prepare to make entry into the house. The suspect, surrounded and subjected to withering gunfire anytime he showed his face in a window, had by now set the house on fire. Also pictured are, from left to right, officers John McKay, Gary Conwell, Norris Jones, Tom Dinardo, and Capt. Billy Miller. (Courtesy of the *Kokomo Tribune*.)

Police remove the body of accused drug dealer Robert Gray, 12 hours after he detonated a bomb in the sheriff's office. SWAT officers Gary Guest (second from left) and Rick Nutt (right) responded to the bombing and assisted investigators John Cardwell (left) and Tom Melton (second from right) with the crime scene. Gray may have intended to murder a police informant in the circuit courtroom during his trial. (Courtesy of the *Kokomo Tribune*.)

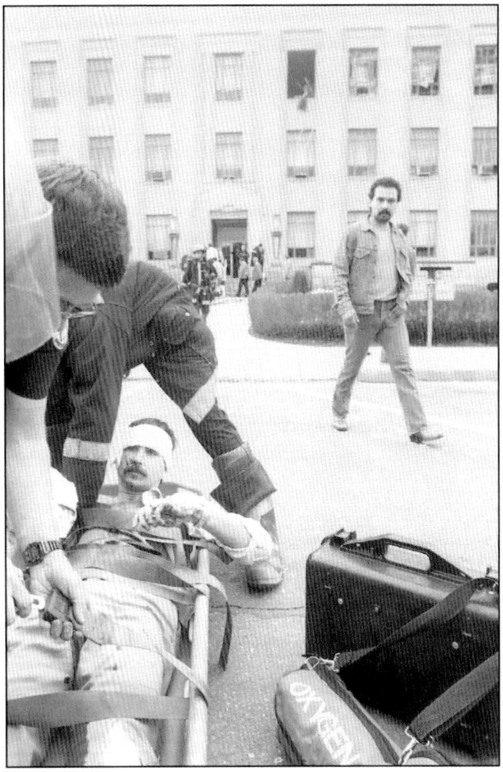

Sheriff's deputy Don Howard received emergency first-aid treatment on the street in front of the courthouse. Howard was among the most seriously injured of the 15 people hurt in the bombing. Narcotics detective Jack Adams of the Kokomo police and detective Joe Coate of the Indiana State Police were both injured by flying debris while waiting to testify against Robert Gray. Kokomo police narcotics detective Bobby Salinas (right) is also pictured. (Courtesy of the *Kokomo Tribune*.)

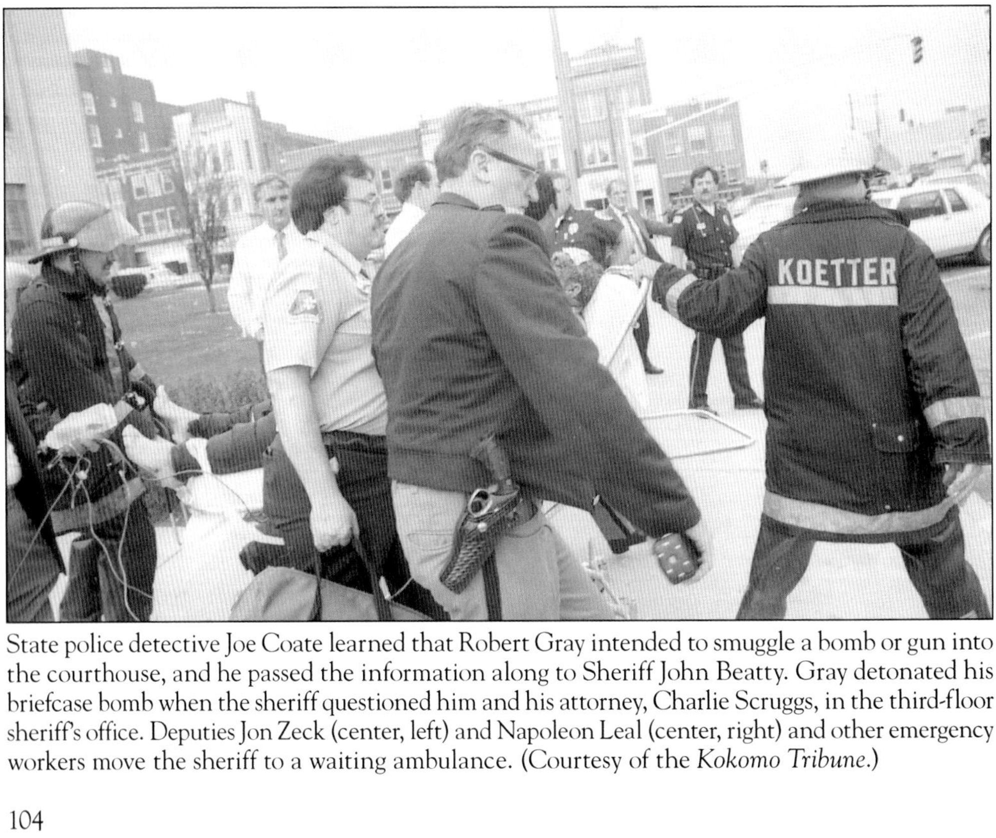

State police detective Joe Coate learned that Robert Gray intended to smuggle a bomb or gun into the courthouse, and he passed the information along to Sheriff John Beatty. Gray detonated his briefcase bomb when the sheriff questioned him and his attorney, Charlie Scruggs, in the third-floor sheriff's office. Deputies Jon Zeck (center, left) and Napoleon Leal (center, right) and other emergency workers move the sheriff to a waiting ambulance. (Courtesy of the *Kokomo Tribune*.)

Deputies Larry Shipman (left) and Mark Fisher lead a courthouse worker to safety in the aftermath of the bombing. The suspect, Robert Gray, was on trial for dealing LSD, and he was suspected of trying to blow up his girlfriend's car in 1983 and later shooting her in Marion. His bombing of the Howard County Courthouse changed the nature of courthouse security around the country. (Courtesy of the *Kokomo Tribune*.)

Tom Dinardo completely reorganized the Kokomo police honor guard with new uniforms, mandatory drills, and an official policy that dictated precisely how the unit could be used. Probably unnoticed by the casual observer, the stripe on the uniform trousers was applied with red stitching, to recognize the many sacrifices of local officers throughout the history of the police department. Dinardo (standing, fourth from left) later served as chief of police. (Courtesy of Kokomo Police Department.)

Here, police and sheriff deputies participated in the Law Enforcement Torch Run to benefit Special Olympics. Officers are required to either donate directly or to solicit donations before they can register for the run, from Kokomo to the Notre Dame campus in South Bend. The run is thought to be the biggest and most successful grassroots fundraising effort in the United States. (Courtesy of Lynn Rudolph.)

Efforts to diversify the police department during the administration of Chief Rodger Fain included hiring more female officers. Mayor Steve Daily administers the oath of honor and code of ethics to Kim Powell (left) and Linda Cothern. Also pictured are Mark Miller, Sean Kinney, Joe Culbertson, and Anthony Alexander. (Courtesy of Lynn Rudolph.)

Standards for recruiting, selecting, and training Kokomo police officers were implemented under the direction of Chief Fain and Inspector Jay Weir. Applicants to the department could reach eligibility status only after passing a battery of intelligence, physical, and emotional fitness tests. Shown here interviewing an applicant are, from left to right, Weir, Gary Guest, "Robbie" Robertson, and Jerry Harrison. Lt. Cliff Stover (not pictured) was instrumental in developing the recruit-training program, which built upon the academy's basic training.

Recruit officers who completed an orientation and graduated from the Indiana Law Enforcement Academy at Plainfield underwent a 16-week field-training program, culminating in a period of intense supervision. Of the recruits who met academy standards, 20 percent were washed out during their first, probationary year of service. Here, Stan Ridlin (right) trains on the pistol range with Rick Nutt. (Courtesy of Kokomo Police Department.)

A party was held at the courthouse in honor of Bob Daily's service to Howard County as a commissioner. Daily (center) is seen here eating cake with Bob Sargent (left), who served as sheriff from 1975 to 1981, and the current sheriff, Earle Howard. Daily was a successful farmer by trade, and was pressed into serving briefly as the sheriff of Howard County during the last year of Sargent's administration.

Officer Don Whitehead was on his way to investigate an accident when a tanker truck ran a traffic light and rammed his patrol car at Markland Avenue and Apperson Way. A former Greentown deputy marshal, Whitehead would later retire from the Kokomo police to work as a consultant for the US Justice Department. (Courtesy of Marty Talbert.)

Officer Don Bolan (left) and Deputy Craig Trott cover the front of the First National Bank downtown during a late-afternoon robbery. Within minutes, officers had surrounded the block and rousted two likely suspects from the neighborhood. Unfortunately, when the suspects were brought back to the bank for identification, nobody recognized them. The real robber, it seemed, had slipped through the dragnet. (Courtesy of the *Kokomo Tribune*.)

About a half hour later, the robber called the police station and told officers where they could find him. In this photograph, officer Norris Jones leads the suspect away following identification. The same man robbed a Hoffer Street bank a few years later and was again quickly apprehended, leading Lt. John Hurlock to conclude that "arresting this guy for bank robbery is like fishing in a pay pit." (Courtesy of the *Kokomo Tribune*.)

Oscar Cook designed many outstanding buildings in Kokomo, including the Union Bank building, the Elks Club, and the Haynes Stellite Offices, all of which have been demolished. Cook also designed the present county courthouse, which, for some reason, never included a safe area for moving prisoners. The oversight has resulted in several escaped detainees, including these two men, who were quickly captured behind Higbee Body Shop downtown. (Courtesy of the *Kokomo Tribune*.)

It was pretty routine. Deputies Napoleon Leal and Don Howard were answering a call in Indian Heights. As they pulled in front and started together up the snow-covered sidewalk, Michael Phillips came outside. This wasn't going to be a typical family fight, in which the officers could talk the husband into taking a walk around the block. The man was waving a shotgun and threatening to kill his girlfriend. (Courtesy of the *Kokomo Tribune*.)

Deputy Dennis Vondersaar arrived on the scene, and he and Leal snuck up on Phillips from the back of the house. There was little in the way of cover, and when Phillips started shooting, Vondersaar was struck in the hand. Leal was more seriously injured. Deputy J.D. Beatty was wounded in a second exchange of gunfire. Vondersaar is seen here at the jail after the shooting. (Courtesy of the *Kokomo Tribune*.)

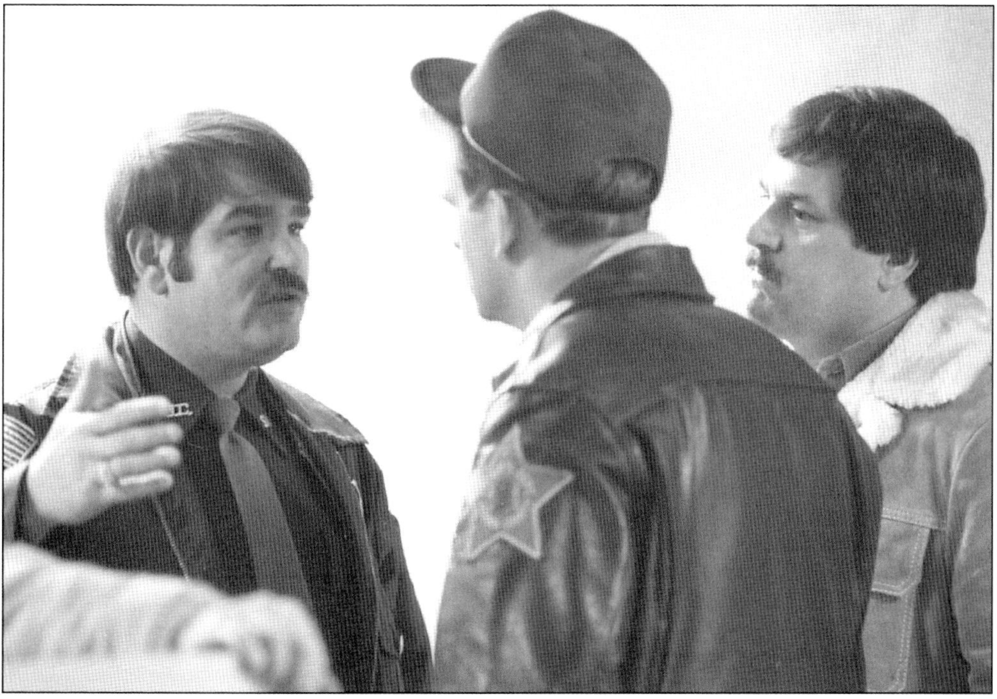

The sheriff's SWAT team arrived at the scene and fired tear gas into the house after trying unsuccessfully to talk Phillips outside. Phillips came to the door again with his shotgun and was fatally wounded in an exchange of gunfire with the deputies. Here, Jim Stitt (left) briefs fellow deputies Jerry Marr (center) and Jerry Jumper after the tragic incident. (Courtesy of the *Kokomo Tribune*.)

The Howard County Sheriff's Department began issuing patrol cars as part of the deputies' basic equipment in the 1950s, when manpower limitations made 24-hour patrol coverage impossible. Deputies were often called out from home. In this photograph, off-duty sergeant Roger Smith (center) discovered a safe that was taken from a Kokomo burglary and dumped alongside a country road. Deputy Craig Trott (right) and Kokomo police detective Jeff Kirk have responded to investigate. (Courtesy of Kokomo Police Department.)

Officer Dan Groves was lured into an ambush following the anonymous complaint of a traffic accident at Union Street and Markland Avenue. Police cordoned off the neighborhood and began a door-to-door search after the suspect ran off with Groves's handgun. Dead of an apparent self-inflicted gunshot wound, the suspect was located in the 900 block of South Locke Street that afternoon. Officer Groves was not seriously injured. (Courtesy of the *Kokomo Tribune*.)

The Peacemakers began as a fellowship of Christian police officers. They used their unique spiritual song stylings to deliver a message of hope. Greg Davis (second from left) proposed and implemented the police chaplaincy program, which offered counseling to officers and their families and assisted the police department's new Victims Assistance Program. Shown here performing are, from left to right, Mike Wheeler, Davis, Stan Ridlin, Larry Ives, Phil Templin, and Wally Sitzes. (Courtesy of Kokomo Police Department.)

The sheriff's department stopped sponsoring the Law Enforcement Explorer Post, which Sheriff Bob Sargent had organized in the 1970s. Jerry Williams had benefited from the program as an explorer. As a Kokomo police officer, he reorganized the post under the umbrella of the Police Athletic League's many and increasingly diverse youth programs. Cadets are shown here attending an annual awards banquet. (Courtesy of Kokomo Police Department.)

Deputies Steve Russell (behind car) and Roy Phipps work a head-on accident at County Roads 250 East and 100 South. (Courtesy of Marty Talbert.)

Officer Orville Harness (center) and the afternoon watch commander, Capt. Dick Sosbe (right), examine a vehicle that was involved in a head-on crash along the American Legion golf course on Lincoln Road. Lt. John Brown, traffic unit commander, is on the far left, talking with a photographer. (Courtesy of Marty Talbert.)

Six

Hip-Hop

The 1990s

You can't swing a dead cat in this town without knockin' a crack dealer over.

—Narcotics detective Doug Mason

In the late 1980s, Chief Lynn Rudolph furthered his predecessor's efforts toward a more efficient and accountable police department by taking steps to get the Kokomo Police Department accredited by the Commission on Accreditation of Law Enforcement. Over the course of the next 10 years, hundreds of policies were written to codify the way the police department did business. It was a massive undertaking, and many of the new standards were also implemented by the sheriff's department.

The undercover marijuana investigation dubbed Operation Three Amigos was concluded in January 1990, when the body of suspected smuggler Ismael Sanchez was found behind an Ohio Street transmission shop. At the conclusion of the 18-month-long investigation, 24 people were arrested by police officers, deputies, and troopers assigned to the Howard County Drug Task Force. Over the course of three years, Sanchez and his cohorts brought $2.4 million worth of marijuana to Kokomo from Texas.

Technology allowed law enforcement to keep better records and to access data more easily. Kokomo police quickly put this information to work through a crime analysis office that was responsible for collating gun permits with pawn tickets and crime reports, to identify patterns of crime throughout the county. This allowed resources to be assigned appropriately. Officers were assigned to specific neighborhoods and made responsible for community problems on these beats, while a host of new programs linked police with schools and the courts to identify juvenile offenders.

But the biggest challenge to Howard County law enforcement came with the emergence of crack cocaine. As crack dealers fled the violent and oversaturated markets of Detroit, St. Louis, and Memphis, they converged on places like Kokomo, where they often set up elaborate street markets and created an environment of complete lawlessness. Violence followed. By the end of the decade, police officers and sheriff's deputies had formed tactical teams devoted almost completely to executing high-risk search warrants in crack houses.

Michael's Transmission Repair, at 520 North Ohio Street, was seized by the Howard County prosecutor just 10 days into the last decade of the century. A Howard County Drug Task Force investigation, Operation Three Amigos, had netted 24 arrests, including Ismael Sanchez and transmission shop owner Jimmy Michael. Sanchez had disappeared in November and could not be located on the day of the raids. (Courtesy of the *Kokomo Tribune*.)

Acting on information gleaned from those arrested in the raids, police discovered the body of Ismael Sanchez on January 22. He had been murdered by his associates, who dumped his body into an eight-foot grave beneath a collection of old automotive parts. Captain of Detectives Russell Ricks (right) and Det. Sgt. Dave Mitchell work to exhume the body. (Courtesy of The Kokomo Tribune.)

Dignitaries of every stripe flocked to the transmission shop despite the cold, wet January weather. To protect the crime scene from contamination, Inspector Hurlock has permitted only those personnel necessary to the investigation inside. Chief Rudolph (right, in dark jacket and cap) and Mayor Sargent are waiting patiently outside the fence. (Courtesy of The Kokomo Tribune)

Capt. Larkin Fourkiller talks with a motorist during a traffic stop. As commander of the training unit, Fourkiller honed the SWAT team into a precision tactical unit and trained members of the drug task force in high-risk entries and building searches. High-profile drug enforcement, including loud and aggressive search warrant executions, were implemented in a futile attempt to slow down drug trafficking. (Courtesy of Kokomo Police Department.)

Street-drug interdiction teams worked closely with troopers to locate contraband on the busy US 31 corridor. Indiana state trooper Mike Tarrh (center) is assisted during a traffic stop by dog-handler Kevin Scott and interdiction officer Tom Hudson (right). Canine teams never worked alone, because the handler was busy with his dog and found it difficult to keep track of suspects during an inspection. (Courtesy of Kokomo Police Department.)

It can be tricky to get handcuffs on somebody who seriously does not want to be arrested. The struggle to restrain a suspect often boils down to a question of endurance, or of elevating the level of force. That is why officers will swarm a combative individual, in an attempt to affect the arrest with minimal injury. This burglary suspect was arrested after holding a knife to his own throat and trying to bargain for his escape. (Courtesy of the *Kokomo Tribune*.)

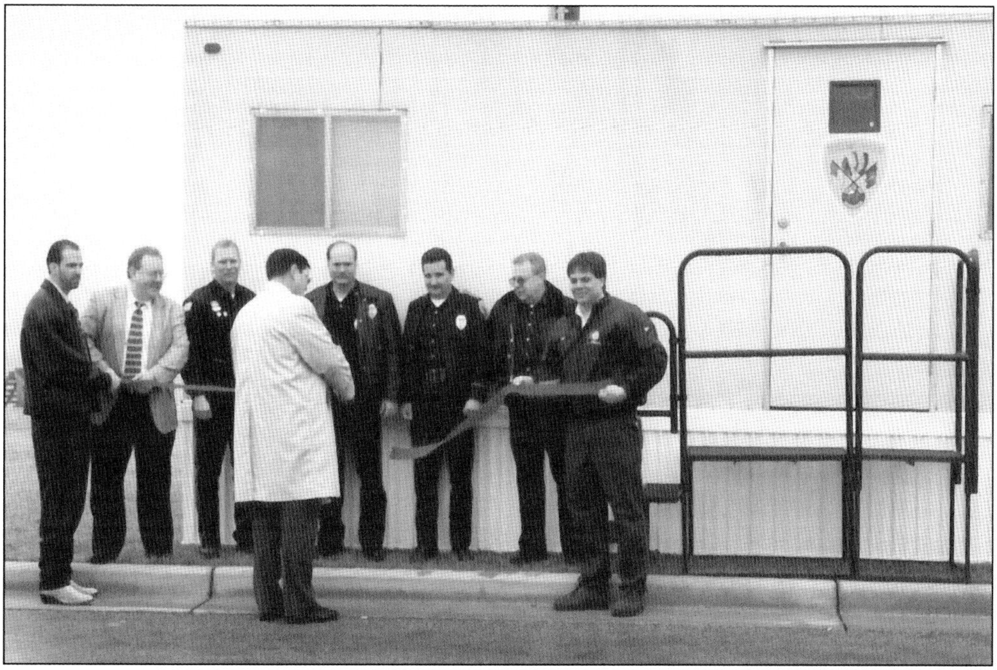

As Markland Avenue east of US 31 grew into a vibrant retail center, Walmart sponsored a police substation in its parking lot. Pictured here at the ribbon cutting are Walmart officials and, from left to right, officer Linke Catron, Sgt. Dave Mitchell, officer Jim Cook, and patrol division commander, Capt. Mike Cody. Chief Charlie Hackett holds the ceremonial scissors. (Courtesy of Kokomo Police Department.)

Many military traditions exist in modern policing, including the hand salute, rendered only in formal situations as a gesture of respect. Here, Kokomo Police Honor Guard members, from far left to right, Tonda Cockrell, Dave Galloway, and Troy Hintz salute Chief Carlie Hackett (not in uniform) as he leaves the city council chambers after a change of command ceremony upon his retirement. Also pictured are, from left to far right, Det. Sean Kinney, Annabelle Hackett, and Asst. Chief Russell Ricks. (Courtesy of Kokomo Police Department.)

Officer Mark Clark investigates a traffic accident at Washington Street and Lincoln Road while a wrecker hooks up. Whether or not the price of gasoline had any effect on the incidence of motor vehicle accidents in Howard County is unknown. (Courtesy of Kokomo Police.)

Law and Order magazine chose the Kokomo police as the best-dressed police department in America for a city with less than 200 officers. Capt. Larkin Fourkiller entered the department's nomination: "Our uniforms are worn proudly and are a symbol of excellent service provided on behalf of an outstanding community." (Courtesy of Kokomo Police.)

The popularity of crack cocaine in 1993 drew drug dealers into the streets and changed the nature of drug enforcement forever. Aggressive enforcement was often resented by neighborhood residents, resulting in confrontations and violence. Patrol officers here have responded to East Madison Street after narcotics officers made several arrests. (Courtesy of Kokomo Police.)

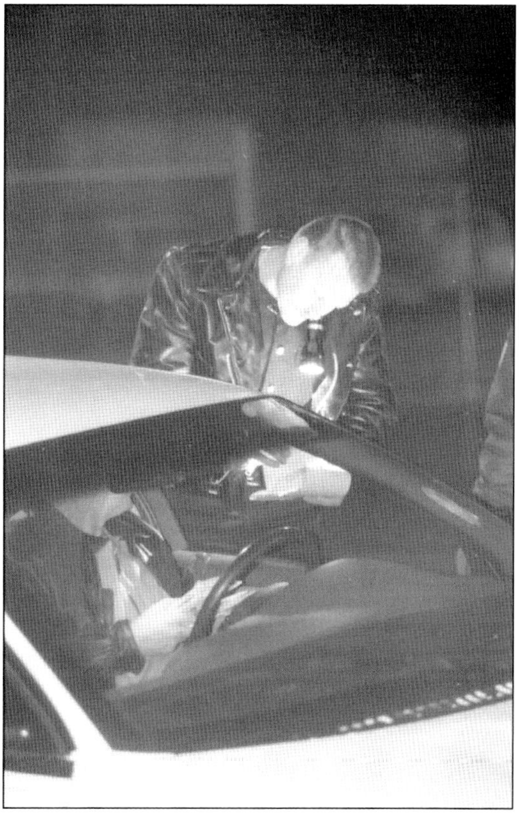

Crack cocaine dealers fled the violence and oversaturated drug markets of Chicago, St. Louis, and Indianapolis for small communities like Kokomo. Uniformed street-drug interdiction teams were comprised of extremely courteous officers with a thorough understanding of search and seizure laws and targeted street-level dealers and their customers. Officer Doug Mason is pictured. (Courtesy of Kokomo Police.)

Canine teams were one of several new programs that were born during the violence of the early 1970s. While trained to sniff out some illegal drugs, the teams were used mostly for patrol and crowd control and the program was abandoned in 1978. The 1990s surge in drug-related crime fueled interest in reviving the program, and canine teams were routinely paired with an interdiction officer. During the same period, the sheriff's department formed a bomb-sniffing dog team. (Courtesy of the *Kokomo Tribune*.)

By the end of the decade, drug trafficking and the accompanying violence was answered with more resources. Chief Charlie Hackett, Sheriff Jerry Marr, and Prosecutor James Fleming grew the Drug Task Force to six agents, including sheriff's department sergeant Roger Smith and state police detective Larry Mote, two canine teams, two uniform interdiction teams, and three full-time prosecutors. Pictured are, from left to right, (first row) the author, Tom Hudson, and Rick Nutt; (second row) Deric Beroshock, Roger Smith, Doug Mason, Dave Foster, and Mike Wheeler. (Courtesy of Kokomo Police Department.)

Deputy Sheriff Jon Zeck, currently retired from law enforcement, has spent most of his career researching the history of the public safety agencies serving Howard County. In this photograph, Zeck is showing circuit court judge Lynn Murray one of the Thompson submachine guns in the Kokomo Police inventory. Delicately maintained by the training division, these fully functional relics are part of the legacy. (Courtesy of Kokomo Police Department.)

The potato famine of the 1840s brought thousands of Irish immigrants to the United States, where many of the men were hired as policemen. Consequently, the funeral for an officer brings out the Irish community, which honors its fallen countrymen with traditional and mournful bagpipes. Officers Wilber Lewis (left) and Tonda Cockrell kept the tradition alive with their colorful uniforms and Scottish pipes, which are played because they are louder than Irish bagpipes. (Courtesy of Jon Zeck.)

Officers Wil Lewis (left) and Shawn Haus have lowered the national colors to half-staff in honor of fellow police officers who have lost their lives in the line of duty. The ceremony is conducted at Kokomo City Hall during National Police Week, the week of May 15, as dedicated by Pres. John Kennedy in 1962. The Kokomo Police Department and Howard County Sheriff's Department began to formally recognize the event in 1988. (Courtesy of Kokomo Police Department.)

Drug interdiction teams usually worked in uniform, to provide a highly visible deterrence to street crime. But they were encouraged to suggest their own operations, adjust their working hours, and dress appropriately for whatever they were doing. Here, Tom Hudson (left) and Dave Foster check a car near Purdum and Madison Streets. Officers often used the vacant house in the background to monitor street activity. (Courtesy of Kokomo Police Department.)

The police departments of Greentown and Russiaville are, in a way, the in-laws of Howard County's law enforcement family. Nevertheless, they are an integral part of public safety. Pictured here are Greentown marshal Jeff Bennett (left) and Russiaville marshal Roger Wadell.

Police officers hold season tickets to the greatest show on Earth. Any account of how police officers perform their jobs should include a discussion of what the job does to police officers. Here, Teresa Galloway and Greg Baldini sort out a disturbance on the midnight shift. (Courtesy of Kokomo Police Department.)

Officer Chad Van Camp stopped along East Sycamore Street when a man flagged him down to report a robbery. Seconds later, Van Camp was in the middle of a shoot-out that started because of an unpaid dope debt. While Deputy Keith Myers provides cover, Det. Mike Banush (center) and Van Camp drag a shooting victim out of the line of fire. (Courtesy of the *Kokomo Tribune*.)

Officers Craig Musgrave and Teresa Kelley forged a relationship as classmates at the Indiana Law Enforcement Academy. While investigating a narcotics complaint four years later, the two officers were ambushed in the dark, second-floor stairwell of an East Sycamore Street apartment house. Only through their mutual courage and commitment to one another were both officers able to survive. Their story is typical of what police officers do, and have always done, for the Howard County community. (Courtesy of Kokomo Police Department.)

LAW ENFORCEMENT CODE OF ETHICS

As a Law Enforcement Officer, my fundamental duty is to serve mankind; to safeguard lives and property; to protect the innocent against deception, the weak against oppression or intimidation, and the peaceful against violence or disorder; and to respect the Constitutional rights of all men to liberty, equality and justice.

I will keep my private life unsullied as an example to all; maintain courageous calm in the face of danger, scorn, or ridicule; develop self-restraint; and be constantly mindful of the welfare of others. Honest in thought and deed in both my personal and official life, I will be exemplary in obeying the laws of the land and the regulations of my department. Whatever I see or hear of a confidential nature or that is confided to me in my official capacity will be kept ever secret unless revelation is necessary in the performance of my duty.

I will never act officiously or permit personal feelings, prejudices, animosities or friendships to influence my decisions. With no compromise for crime and with relentless prosecution of criminals, I will enforce the law courteously and appropriately without fear or favor, malice or ill will, never employing unnecessary force or violence and never accepting gratuities.

I recognize the badge of my office as a symbol of public faith, and I accept it as a public trust to be held as long as I am true to the ethics of the police service. I will constantly strive to achieve these objectives and ideals, dedicating myself before God to my chosen profession . . . law enforcement.

The International Association of Chiefs of Police first developed this code of ethics in 1957. Revised in 1989, the Law Enforcement Code of Ethics, sometimes called the Code of Honor, was not adopted until 1991. Thousands of law enforcement officers have dedicated themselves to these noble ideals.

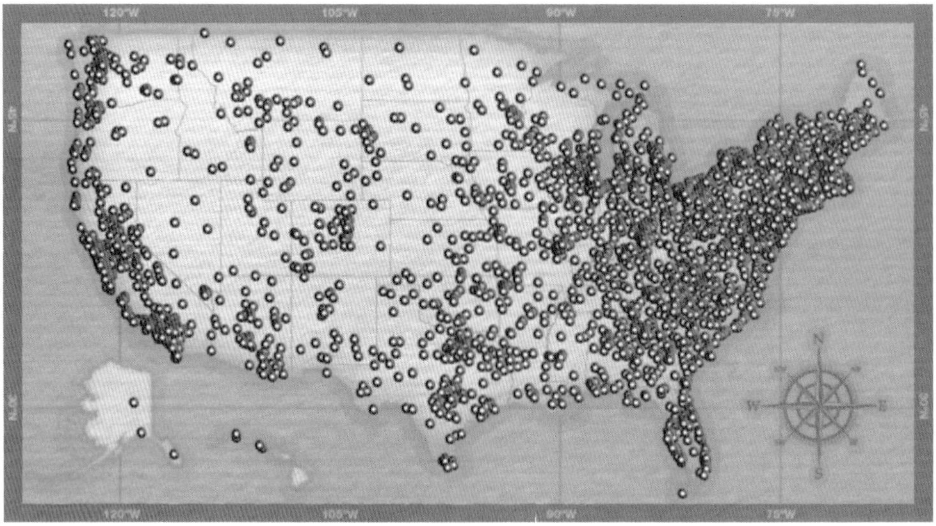